Praise for *By the Iowa Sea*
A Best Book of the Year — *Library Journal* and *BookPage* 2012

"A memoirist with a poet's soul, [Blair] takes what is arguably the most mercilessly exploited natural resource in all of literature and replenishes it. Blair has an autistic son, Michael . . . it is their love story, more than that between Blair and his wife, that lends the tempest and its longed-for destructiveness their emotional valence, and this memoir its observational virtuosity."
—*The New York Times Book Review*

"Eloquently gritty."
—*Elle*

"Blair put away his motorcycle and his dreams to do manual labor while supporting four children, one of whom is autistic. Rekindling a sense of purpose took something big: a terrible flood. Not a whiny work; fresh, plainspoken, and down-to-earth. Definitely try."
—*Library Journal*

"Blair's thoughtful memoir displays the strengths and resilience of committed lovers in a tumultuous relationship."
—*Publishers Weekly*

"Joe is a refrigeration technician (a pipe fitter) as well as an aspiring writer (this is his first book, and it is very well written). He takes the reader into very personal aspects of his life, including a brief encounter with another woman. When the river floods, it indirectly causes Joe and his wife to delve more deeply into their lives and face their fears and concerns."
—*Washington Missourian*

"Blair demonstrates how dramatic and even symbolic commonplace moments can be."
—*Tampa Bay Times*

"Engrossing, thoughtful, startlingly honest, and, ultimately, hopeful, *By the Iowa Sea* may be Blair's first book, but I hope—and fully expect—it will not be his last."

—*Iowa City Press Citizen*

"An intimate, startling memoir that honors and elevates our quotidian existence. With his contagious curiosity as to what drives him and what holds him back, Blair writes fearlessly and beautifully about the family he loves and also betrays, the people he treasures and plots to escape from. *By the Iowa Sea* is funny and unsettling, painful and rock-and-roll romantic, and it has the invigorating ring of truth on every page."

—Scott Spencer, author of *Endless Love* and *Man in the Woods*

"Joe Blair portrays family life and his own emotional life with tremendous courage and a searing honesty. I admired the prose and the story as I read. I finished the book admiring the man."

—Chris Offutt, author of *The Same River Twice*

"*By the Iowa Sea* is a sometimes angry, often startling, and always riveting journey through infidelity, drinking, storms, work, beauty, and the simultaneous frustration and sublimity of raising a disabled child. Blair's writing is vivid, his subjects are heartbreaking, and his ending is flat-out gorgeous."

—Anthony Doerr, author of *Memory Wall*

"Joe Blair's passion and courage are evident on each page of *By the Iowa Sea*. He is among those rare writers brave enough to risk everything for his work, and the result is this hypnotic, electrifying book."

—Alexander Maksik, author of *You Deserve Nothing*

"A devastating flood provides the backdrop for Joe Blair's moving memoir about crisis and change. If you want to understand how a good man can resolve the conflict between his youthful dreams and his adult sense of duty, read this book. His honesty about the real challenges of marriage and parenting is startling in the best sense, and shot through with refreshing humor."

—Julie Metz, author of the *New York Times*–
bestselling memoir *Perfection*

"Joe Blair writes with uncommon openness and pain about the pleasures and difficulties of marriage. He also conjures the beauty of the Iowa landscape—even under water. *By the Iowa Sea* includes one of the most touchingly funny sex scenes—or should I say, non-sex scenes—I've read. I am sure women and men will respond to his voice."

—Anne Taylor Fleming, author of *Marriage: A Duet* and
As If Love Were Enough

"Joe Blair's voice is uncommonly perceptive, startlingly honest, and powerfully moving. This is eloquence born of pain, sharpened by humor, and burnished, finally, by understanding and redemption."

—Ethan Canin, author of *Emperor of the Air* and *America, America*

By the Iowa Sea

A Memoir

Joe Blair

SCRIBNER

New York London Toronto Sydney New Delhi

Scribner
A Division of Simon & Schuster, Inc.
1230 Avenue of the Americas
New York, NY 10020

Certain names and identifying characteristics have been changed
and certain characters and events have been compressed or reordered.

First Scribner trade paperback edition March 2013

SCRIBNER and design are registered trademarks of The Gale Group, Inc., used under license by
Simon & Schuster, Inc., the publisher of this work.

For information about special discounts for bulk purchases, please contact Simon & Schuster
Special Sales at 1-866-506-1949 or business@simonandschuster.com.

The Simon & Schuster Speakers Bureau can bring authors to your live event. For more
information or to book an event, contact the Simon & Schuster Speakers Bureau at
1-866-248-3049 or visit our website at www.simonspeakers.com.

Designed by Leydiana Rodríguez-Ovalles

Manufactured in the United States of America

10 9 8 7 6 5 4 3 2 1

Library of Congress Control Number: 2011038073

ISBN 978-1-4516-3605-5
ISBN 978-1-4516-3606-2 (pbk)
ISBN 978-1-4516-3607-9 (ebook)

Permissions appear on page 279.

I cannot tell how Eternity seems. It sweeps around me like a sea . . .

—Emily Dickinson

By the Iowa Sea

Part One

IT BEGINS WITH RAIN. An innocent enough thing. Rain and rain and rain. Day after day of it. Through February and March and April and May. Forcing us to seek out shelters that will soon, in some cases, be transformed into pontoon boats. While the rain beats down on the roofs of Iowa City and Cedar Rapids and Marengo and Oxford Junction like bouncing hammers, the unstoppable thing is happening. Rivers rise up out of their banks, lifting our neat little split-entry lives from their foundations, tearing away electrical hookups and gas hookups and phone lines, bringing us to a place where there are no riverbanks and no street names and nothing else that resembles a city. The rivers will become oceans. And Deb and I will become not lost in the oceans but a part of them: suddenly vast. Subordinate to none. Scooping and hungry.

The wind comes unevenly in cold down-rushes and everyone at the Coral Ridge Mall knows that something unusual is about to happen. If the raindrops were chickens or pancakes, I don't think we would be surprised. Because anything is possible. The small trees outside Barnes & Noble are showing the undersides of their leaves, their branches confused as to which way to go, pushing downward and then upward and then twisting clockwise. People are gathered in the very place the voice on the intercom tells us not to gather: in front of the large plate-glass windows. We can see everything from here. The crosswalk sign bending sideways. The racing

3

clouds. But it isn't enough for me. I want to be *in* the storm. I want to smell it and hear the wind and feel the first enormous raindrops hit my skin. I'm hungry for that.

I push through the heavy doors and wait outside the entrance. The storm excites me. It excites us all. Even though we have worried expressions on our faces, we don't move from the windows. Because we want the change to come. We all want it. We are on our phones to wives or husbands or children. "Are you in the basement?" "Stay inside!" "Stay away from the windows!" These are the things we say. The sky looks the way ocean waves must look from the bottom of the sea. We are starfish looking up at the waves. And it intrigues us that there is such power in the world. Power enough to twist trees like corkscrews. To rip us all up by the roots.

A blast of wind staggers me. I catch myself from falling by grabbing the crosswalk sign, itself less than stable, oscillating wildly on its channeled steel post. One drop, the size of my hand, in the middle of the crosswalk. Another drop somewhere on the sidewalk. Then hundreds of drops all at once. Then thousands. Falling hard. Drawn to the ground as if by magnetic force. I step back beneath the entrance, afraid. The hunched figure of a woman rushes through one of the double doors clutching a paper bag to her chest and holding one hand over her head, as if to keep her wig on. "Smells like rain!" she shouts over the sound of the mad charge of water from the sky as she bustles past me into the storm. I smile. I take a deep breath. And then I laugh. Because she's right. It does smell like rain.

THE SOUND OF ENTHUSIASTIC APPLAUSE. Rain. I shout to Deb from the kitchen, but there's no need to shout. She knows I'm leaving. Maybe she opens her eyes and checks the glowing red digits on the clock radio. It's 5:45 in the morning and I know she's not getting out of bed for another half hour, when she'll need to get Sam and William and Lucy up and then, after the boys take their showers, she'll need to give Mike his bath and dress him for school. She certainly isn't getting up now. I don't blame her. And you don't see me rushing back up the stairs for my good-bye kiss.

I grab my lunch from the refrigerator and head for my truck. My lunch consists of one piece of Hy-Vee fried chicken, which I've sealed in a Ziploc bag, and a few potato chips, which I've also sealed in a Ziploc bag, both jammed into a brown paper sack. There's also a clementine. But there isn't a note. When we were first married, Deb made my lunches and she'd slip notes in the bag: "I love you, sweetheart!" or "I'll miss you!" And there'd be a sketch of some kind. Maybe a nude figure. Or a cat. Or a tree. Or a heart with an arrow.

The sound of a door slamming. Deb can guess what the next sound will be: the sound of my work truck pulling out of the driveway. The pause. The shift. The revving of an engine. The splashing of a puddle. The fading roar. These are the sounds of my leaving. It's something she's heard every day for sixteen years. From her bed. From the kitchen. From the bathroom. From the laundry room. Joe leaving. Joe leaving. Joe leaving. Joe leaving. Joe leaving. Joe leaving. Joe leaving. (That's a week's worth.)

Deb doesn't make any sound at all by staying. I never drive away and think, There's that sound again. Because there is no sound.

I drive down the hill on River Street and take a left on Rocky Shore, which runs along the Iowa River, normally a modest-looking strip of water but now looking anything but modest, rather a wild set of rapids rebelling against the banks that have constricted it for so long. The river is not what we thought it was. It's threatening to overrun the little picnic table and benches where we rest on our walks, and the grill in the park by the railroad overpass. I'm heading for Luther College, about 125 miles north of Iowa City, where I need to respond to a service call and complete my spring inspection of the air-conditioning equipment. I take a right under the railroad overpass beside the Coralville Strip while Deb lies in bed, the glowing red digits blinking.

THIS SPRING HAS BEEN especially dour. Not so much a new season as the shadow of the preceding one. It has sleeted a lot. And rained. Every day it has rained. And the sun has rarely broken through. Everyone complains about the crappy spring. And the guys on the news never stop talking about the possibility of an impending flood. They seem happy about it. Grateful, maybe, for something to report.

The rain has already brought the insects out and my windshield is streaked with them. Tens of thousands of bugs have met their death against the front end of my GMC cargo van. It doesn't bother me much when, on the south side of Independence near the cemetery, a butterfly gets tangled up in my wiper blade. I'm not a big insect lover. It doesn't break my heart to see a butterfly die. The entrance to the cemetery is a high, galvanized steel gate with fancy, leafy designs decorating the arch. "Mount Hope," it says. I wonder about that name. I wonder who, exactly, is supposed to be hoping and what, exactly, they're supposed to be hoping for.

Elton John sings about butterflies being free. "Butterflies are free to fly." This is what he sings. And then he wonders why the butterflies fly away. It's a touching sentiment I suppose. Bugs being free. But a bug being free doesn't mean very much to me. What do bugs do with all that freedom anyway?

The pair of choppers rolling along ahead of me appear to be loaded down for a long trip. One guy, burly and bearded, who looks like his name might be Rusty, wears a black do-rag and Oakley sunglasses with bright yellow lenses. He's riding a Harley Panhead, a classic bike. The same type of bike Peter Fonda rode in *Easy Rider*. The other guy, more slender and also bearded, who might be named Butch, wears nothing at all on his head. That's how free he is. He's riding a newer Harley Softtail with the Blockhead engine. The women on the backs, one who might be Sheila and the other who might be Cassie, look comfortable enough. They're both dressed in black chaps and black leather jackets. They lean against their backrests. The Harley guys cruise along slowly the way Harley guys do. I pull up closer to find out where they're from. Minnesota. They must be heading back home. They've each packed a tent. The rest of their gear is wrapped in what look like shower curtains.

The temperature was forecast to reach the mid-seventies, but it can't be much over sixty-five now. One of the women, it might be Sheila, tucks her hands beneath her hair and lifts her elbows up above her head. It will be another day. There's sports talk on AM 1600. The ESPN guys are discussing the Yankees' pitching rotation. It's spring. It's nothing but spring. The rain has ceased for the moment, but there is a bank of dark clouds like scoops of black raspberry ice cream to the north.

I recall Deb being on the back of my motorcycle. And the backrest I built for her because Honda didn't make a backrest for the ST1100 in '91. I have an image of her hunkering down behind me to get out of the wind. The telephone poles flicking by and those old concrete-and-cable guardrails like crooked rows of snuffed-out cigarettes and the barns gliding slowly along on the horizon like ghosts. Maybe it was a mistake for Deb to get on the back of my motorcycle. It gave me all the control. Maybe this was the first thing she lost to me. But it must have been what she wanted at the time. Or maybe she climbed on simply because she was afraid to take the Honda V35 I had bought her. It was, after all, an ambitious notion, to ride all the way across the country on her own motorcycle when she couldn't even make it up the ramp on the ferry to Martha's Vineyard and that stranger had to come and help her lift the bike off its side and push it up. I had ridden right up onto the ferry and parked my bike. I didn't even notice she had fallen. She wept on the ride over to the island and I stood next to her on the deck drinking my coffee from my Styrofoam cup watching the water. She wouldn't tell me whether she was crying because I hadn't helped her when she fell or because she had lost confidence in her newfound motorcycle riding skills. She told me she wouldn't ride on her own anymore. I laughed. She told me she was serious. But I didn't take her seriously. She left her bike on the Vineyard, and my twin brother, Dave, picked it up later that summer and rode it home.

And so, when it came time for the mighty cross-country motorcycle trip that Deb and I had been planning, she was right where she wanted to be. On the back of my motorcycle. We had been talking about it since that day we sat in the U Lowell cafeteria and she told me she was from Minnesota and I drew a floor plan for a house on a napkin and said maybe we could go west and be homesteaders. And there we were. Deb hunkering down behind me to get out of the wind. It was nice, day after day. Nothing to do but climb on the bike and ride. The wildflowers flaring up and dying away and the small clearings and dense forests and lakes and cheap diners and lowly motels along the seldom-used rural routes we took deeper and deeper into the country.

Joe Blair

Everything was new because our love was new and each place seemed like it was more beautiful than the one before. North Dakota was beautiful because it was so flat and clean and because we had never seen anything like it before. And no one could doubt the beauty of Minnesota, the deep pine forests and glacial lakes. But none of this prepared us for Iowa. Nothing was as beautiful as Iowa. In my art appreciation class at UMass Lowell, I remember thinking that Grant Wood must have smoked some powerful weed in order to paint landscapes the way he did, with his roly-poly hills and lollipop trees. I didn't know that such a landscape could exist.

We rode the ST1100 up a gravel road that rose and fell like a roller coaster. Barbed-wire fences along either side, crooked and falling down in places. Farmhouses neat and disheveled. Cattle and hogs. Corn and beans. One run-down farmhouse with an enormous maple tree out front that was at its peak color, so bright it looked like someone had plugged it in. I pulled the motorcycle over on the highest point in the gravel road just past the run-down farmhouse with the miraculous tree and shut off the engine and we got off the bike and walked out into the field. Just walked out into it. Most of the corn had been harvested and we could see for miles out over the oceanic land and far out, maybe a mile away, we could see the smallest house I had ever seen, maybe a one-room schoolhouse. There were no roads that we could see leading to the place and no vegetation surrounding it the way there usually is for a break against the wind. At first, we talked about buying the run-down farmhouse we had passed on the gravel road, a shambling place with a wide front porch and a couch on it and a roof badly in need of repair, but we knew that the farmhouse was well out of our price range. "What about that place?" I said, motioning toward the tiny one-room schoolhouse. Deb was horrified. But she said something along the lines of "Sure. Why couldn't we live in a place like that?" because she knew how I was. I was the sort of guy who liked to imagine doing ridiculous things like buying shacks to live in. So, she had learned to let me imagine these things all I wanted. Then, she'd just sit back and wait for the real world to nibble at the edges of my fantastic dreams and nibble and nibble and, before you knew it, the dreams were gone and what was left was renting an apartment. If Deb took me seriously, it would wear her out. "Yeah," I said. "Why couldn't we?"

We had no way of knowing how things would turn out. The four children. The diagnosis of autism for our third son, Michael. And everything thereafter. Going on and on. It's hard to believe, now, that anyone could inspire such passion in me as Deb did when we were young. That two people could just get on a bike like that and go. Without jobs. Without much money. Without anything really. Except the desire to go.

Somehow, a large vehicle has worked its way between the choppers and me. It's a one-ton F-350 towing a white fifth wheel with the cartoon of a kangaroo on the back. The wind is playing tricks on my dead butterfly. The antennae appear to be moving. The orange and black of the wings are the team colors of the Baltimore Orioles. I look for the bikers. I can still see them up ahead of the kangaroo camper.

I again glance at my butterfly and realize with a tiny start that it's not the wind animating the antennae. They're actually moving on their own, curling and uncurling. I assume it must be some quirk of the nervous system. Like those chickens you hear so much about that run around with their heads chopped off.

Joe Blair

One time, Deb bought me an illustrated book about a little caterpillar named Stripe. It was one of those children's books that are designed to move you to tears by the revelation of some large yet simple truth. There are lots of those types of books regarding the miraculous transformation from hairy worm to butterfly. But really, if you discount the wings, a butterfly looks a lot like a hairy worm.

On impulse, I slow down and pull into a gravel drive in Festina, a town that, as far as I can tell, consists of five or six houses, a bar called the Zipper, an auto body shop called Neal's, and a closed-down car wash. I'm sure the butterfly is dead. There's no way a little tiny thing like that could survive colliding with a big thing like my truck at highway speeds.

I'm not yet at a full stop when the butterfly unfastens itself from my wiper blade and flies away toward Neal's Auto Body. I'm so surprised, I shout. Something like "Hey!" And I let out a bark of laughter. The butterfly seems to flutter its wings a little awkwardly at first. Like maybe it's been damaged. But butterflies aren't the most graceful fliers anyway. So it's hard to tell. For some reason, I'm delighted. Overjoyed.

It's hard to cry. It's especially hard to cry about a butterfly. Ninety-nine percent of me does not want to cry. Ninety-nine percent wants to withhold it. But some things are stronger than the things we want. I guess most things are.

WHEN I REACH DECORAH, I stop at the Family Table for breakfast. An older woman with shockingly pale blue eyes takes my order. I've been coming to this restaurant for over fifteen years. It hasn't changed much. The prices haven't even changed. You can still get two eggs, two links, two pancakes, two strips of bacon, and a cup of coffee for around six bucks. Everything is pretty much the same as always. Decorah has magically escaped the fate of so many other small midwestern towns, which have slowly capitulated to the realities of the modern world, grinding down to nothing more than a few dozen houses and a Casey's General Store, the small diner closed down, the hardware store forsaken, the old banks and community centers lining Main Street simply waiting for the mortar to erode so the bricks can go ahead and collapse. Luther College, in many people's opinion, is largely responsible for the vitality of the town. It lends an air of legitimacy. The remote and noble idea of education gives everyone a good reason to keep trying.

When I finish breakfast, I stop in at the Luther College maintenance shop for a service set of keys and then drive to the Valders science building, where people have been complaining that the biology lab is too warm. After doing some checking, I find that the air-conditioning system that serves the space is short of refrigerant. I leak-test the condensing unit and, unable to find anything, trace the refrigerant lines through the outside wall and into a room directly adjacent to the biology lab. I burst into the room, tool pouch in hand, without knocking and realize that I have burst into a professor's private office. I apologize and tell the professor that I'm working on getting his air-conditioning going again. When I tell people this, they usually cut me a lot of slack because they're so grateful. But this guy just frowns as though he's puzzled by what I've just said. I apologize again and I'm about to leave when he says, "You need to get in there?" He jabs his thumb toward a set of white double doors on the south wall. He speaks in a very soft and patient voice. Like a guy trying to calm someone down. He has a full beard and wears thick glasses. He is hunched over a laptop computer. On its screen is a complicated-looking mathematical formula. I hadn't noticed the white doors until he pointed them out. I'm sure that the air handler must be behind them. "Yes, please," I say. He stands and offers to help move the table, which is partially blocking the doors. "No," I say. "I got it. Thanks."

Ignoring me, he moves to the far end of the table and waits for me to grab my end. I shrug, put down my tool pouch, and lift my end. We move the table together. I thank him. He sits back down in front of his complex-looking mathematical formula. I open the white door, leak-test the refrigerant lines that run to and from the air handler, and then stick the probe of my leak detector into the evaporator section. Finding no refrigerant leaks, I button up the unit. I close the white doors, thank the soft-spoken professor guy again, and tell him he should feel some cool air in about fifteen minutes. He smiles and nods slightly, never looking up from his screen.

On my way out to my truck, I notice two women at the far end of the wide, tiled hallway. "So this must be Ezra," says one. The words echo.

By the Iowa Sea

"This is Ezra," says the other who, I now can see, is holding an infant in her arms. I open the door to the parking lot, walk through it, and let it close behind me.

By noon, the sky is seasick, a swirling mass of black and green. Having found a leak on the copper capillary tube that leads to the low-pressure control, and having repaired the leak and charged the system with refrigerant, I have now begun work on another piece of equipment in the mechanical room of the same building. I'm walking across the parking lot, circling around to the back of my truck, when I hear a sharp voice. I glance in that direction. The woman with the infant I had seen earlier is sitting in the driver's seat of a maroon Chevy Citation, which is parked in the small lot near the entrance. The car door is open. The soft-spoken professor guy is standing outside the car door, stooping slightly.

"What?" says the woman. She says this very loudly. "I can't *hear you!*" She says the last two words as though she has always hated the fact that she can't hear him. And that it would be obvious to anyone that the fact that she can't hear him is solid proof of something utterly disgusting about him.

I am not looking at them. I'm trying very hard to appear unconcerned and inattentive. In fact, I have no desire to hear any part of their conversation. But I can't help it.

"No!" she says, still disgusted. "You're not helping! That's my point!"

I climb into my truck and cut a piece of Greenfield from a spool. I climb back out.

"Yes!" she shouts. "It gripes me!" She is fully aware that he doesn't want her to shout, that her shouting hurts him, makes him feel self-conscious and small. "It doesn't help at all!" she continues. "No! No! You're being selfish and self-centered and—" She's loving this. She's been waiting to say it.

I walk toward the science building. I hear a car door slam. An engine revs. I glance back as I open the door. She's driving away. The poor professor bastard is just standing there watching the maroon Citation accelerate out of the parking lot. And then the rain, as if it just remembered something, comes charging down. The professor makes a run for it. I settle in beneath the overhang near the loading dock. After five or ten seconds, the sound of the rain changes. Silence at first. And then a crackling, hail now bouncing white against the blacktop and pinging against the roofs and hoods of the cars with absolute authority. I look at the sickly green sky with admiration. Of course, I want larger hail. Baseballs. Softballs. Grapefruit. Sea monsters. Wooden rowboats that splinter when they hit.

A part of me feels an obligation to go back inside and hug the professor guy. "I know!" I want to say. "Can you believe that shit?" I don't know why his wife is angry with him. Maybe he habitually ignores her. Or maybe he always talks to her like he's trying to calm her down and maybe this drives her crazy. I don't know. But I do know that when he was a kid, playing with his chemistry set, he never imagined biology was going to be like this.

WHEN MY IDENTICAL TWIN BROTHER, Dave, and I were kids, we'd play a game we called Don and Gary. This was a game in which one of us was a guy named Don and the other one was a guy named Gary. We were just two guys who happened to be grown up. And that was the game. We'd assemble blocks on the floor in a rectangular pattern, which represented cars that we could actually sit in, and we'd pretend to wash them and then drive them around. And we'd pretend to go to the grocery store and to the movies and all the places we figured cool guys would actually go if they were real grown-ups. We never pretended to go places like strip joints or seedy bars. We didn't know places like these existed. And even if we did, we wouldn't have understood why anyone would want to go there.

I do remember being confused when our mother explained how babies came into the world. She told us that a man puts his penis in a woman's vagina and then a baby comes out. Even as a child, I knew she was leaving something out. The way she described it, sex was like dressing those little cutout paper dolls with their little cutout paper clothes, where you have to fold tab B and tab A and then the dress was on. I knew there must be more to it.

Joe Blair

Our mother used to read stories to us before we went to bed. *Huckleberry Finn* and *The Deerslayer* and a book called *The Ghost Boat*, about a rowboat that a bunch of kids believed to be haunted and in the end their mom used it as a planter. Everything in our lives seemed interesting and sensible and, for the most part, enjoyable. And then it happened to us, just as it happens to every other boy in the world. I can't remember the details and I don't really want to try, but one of us (Dave or I) figured out how to masturbate and soon both of us were off to the races. The discovery of orgasm marked the end of everything pure and good in our lives. It also marked the end of any primary role that intellect would play in our decision making.

I fell in love serially. I fell in love with Kathy Killalay. She sat in the front row. Never spoke to her even once. In seventh grade, I fell in love with a girl named Judy from the youth group at church, where we smoked cigarettes. Judy seemed unintimidating and I supposed I loved her after all so I asked her on a date. And we went on a date (my mom dropped us off at the movie theater). And then we were supposed to be "going" with each other. But I was already bored with Judy so I fell in love with Tracy Carol. In a handwritten note on a torn-off corner of notebook paper, I asked Tracy Carol if she wanted to "go" with me. I wrote, "Circle yes or no." She wrote in the word "maybe" and circled that. *Maybe*, of course, meant *no*. And for some reason, I never fell out of love with her. I simply fell in love again over the top of my love for Tracy Carol with Colleen Gagnon, one of the first girls to develop breasts in our class. Colleen and I sent suggestive letters to one another, which Colleen's mother intercepted and shared with my mother. I was forbidden to see Colleen anymore, so that was the end of that. Then I fell in love with Amy Burrell who was a Polynesian girl who had been adopted by an elderly couple from our town. Amy Burrell smoked cigarettes and pot and wore a flower in her hair like Billie Holiday. She was in love with a yellow-haired football player who

lifted weights all the time. She was way out of my league, which is probably why I fell in love with her. I never stood a chance there, so I fell in
love with another girl. I can't remember who. These many loves rarely ran
their course. There was a different shape to each relationship. If you could
call them relationships. They'd probably be better described as desperate,
headlong stumblings.

Our mother had bought a *Playboy* magazine because President Carter
had given an interview in which he claimed to have "lust" in his heart.
Believing it to be of some historical significance, she filed the magazine
away in our dad's filing cabinet. It wasn't hard to track down. All we had
to do was look under "P" for *Playboy*. The centerfold, Patti McGuire, had
breasts. She was taking her clothes off in what appeared to be a bar with
a jukebox and neon signs in the windows. I came to know those series
of pictures intimately, and my favorite, the final picture I'd look at before
completing the mission and then filing the magazine away again under
"P," would change on a regular basis, like my favorite song on *Sgt. Pepper*.
In one picture, Patti was holding open her robe, exposing herself while
standing next to the old-fashioned jukebox, and she held her hand in such
a way that her thumb coincided with her nipple so that I couldn't tell if
her nipple was her thumb or her thumb was her nipple. This confused
me. Did a nipple really look like a thumb? I compared this nipple with
other nipples in the magazine. While whacking off, of course. Dave and
I wore that magazine out. Years later, I learned that Patti McGuire had
married Jimmy Connors. And although I wished her well in my heart, I
was injured because I knew I had never stood a chance.

Dave and I were raised on films and novels that celebrated the Rugged
Individualist. An *Easy Rider* poster was taped to our bedroom wall for the
majority of our childhood, right next to the black-light poster of a haunted

Victorian mansion, and the poster of Farrah Fawcett and her amazing areola. Farrah was nice—that famous, tantalizing fold of fabric—and the haunted house was cool enough

but those two choppers . . .

with those cool looking guys, one with a cowboy hat and one with the American flag sewn on the back of his leather jacket . . .

and that blue, airbrushed desert sky . . .

My mother gave me *Zen and the Art of Motorcycle Maintenance* for my fifteenth birthday, and I read it.

And then I read it again.

And then, at sixteen, I took the five hundred dollars I had earned working in an apple orchard and spent it on a Honda CB360T. The tank was candy-apple red and it had a swooping black stripe with white highlights and if you were going downhill and tucked your chin behind the speedometer and odometer, you could do 70 miles per hour and at night the headlight beam looked like wings, shooting out sideways, illuminating the reflective tape on the mailboxes and signs along the road. When the engine seized, I bought a Chilton manual and, with my father's help, rebuilt it. Then I sold the 360 and bought a brand-new Suzuki GS750. Then I sold the Suzuki and bought a used Kawasaki KZ1000, the superbike of the early eighties, a gleaming black killer that could do 155 on a straightaway. Dave had purchased a Honda 45 Magnum and we planned to go on a marathon motorcycle trip in the summer of 1989, but at the last minute Dave dropped out because, he explained, "I fell in love, man." She was a glass artist who had nursed him through the broken nose he suffered when, during a league softball game, a shot to second base took a bad hop. And now, it seemed, Dave and the glass artist were engaged. I congratulated him and, doing my best imitation of the Rugged Individualist, hit the road alone. I was twenty-five. During the two months of my first cross-country motorcycle trip, I fell in love too. Not with a glass artist or with any unattainable woman in a girlie magazine, but with America. This, I thought, as my 1981 Kawasaki KZ1000 and I rolled over the Brooklyn Bridge in midday traffic, was what Whitman saw.

> *O flood tide rushing below me!*
> *O seagulls oscillating their bodies!*
> *O blab of the pave!*
> *O guy on the KZ1000 crossing the Brooklyn Bridge!*

And all that.

After New York City, I headed north and then straight west through all those dying resort towns and dying industrial towns. I thought of William Kennedy's mournful, bedraggled characters. I rolled through beautiful Ohio and thought of Sherwood Anderson. I shot through Minnesota and then up through South Dakota and Wyoming to California, while the prose of Hunter S. Thompson and Jack Kerouac did cartwheels through my mind. I ate apple pie and vanilla ice cream in downtrodden cafeterias just like Kerouac did, and drank cheap beer in biker bars and slept in the cheapest, most forsaken motels. A few times, I spent the night in cornfields or stands of trees adjacent to highway rest stops. I felt at once that nothing could hurt me and everything could touch me. I felt like an infant rocked in the arms of my nation. There was too much beauty in it. I was pummeled in the face with all of the beauty of the land and the sky all day long. It was everywhere. Even in Nevada. Where the small towns were so run-down and sun-baked and paint-peeling and abused-looking, they never failed to make me want to cry for their beauty. Yes, I thought, I would always do this. I would always travel. I thought I had discovered my true calling. I would never cave in to convention. I would never "settle down."

Joe Blair

Then I met Deb.

Somehow, over the years, I have invented and repeated to myself a story regarding the moment I fell in love with my wife. My subconscious, no doubt wanting to forget certain details, has convinced me that I fell in love with Deb on a particular fall day. I tell myself a clean story devoid of seediness. This is how it goes:

It was a rare day when I first met Deb. The sky was too blue and the trees were freshly yellow and orange and there was just enough breath in the wind to stir up the scent of decay. It was the sort of dazzling day that you count. You say, "How many of these days do I have left in my life? Fifty? Ten?" The answer, on this day, would be *none*. This was the only day.

I had parked my motorcycle up by the tire shop on Thorndike Street in Lowell. On foot, coming from an interview for a part-time job at Baynes McKeen Mechanical in Braintree, swinging my helmet by its strap, I made my way toward the Owl Diner. I figured I'd order a celebratory cheeseburger and fries. Celebratory because I had made it back from my cross-country motorcycle trip in time for fall semester at UMass Lowell and now I also had a part-time job. I was clearing the corner near the Owl when I saw her. I thought I had seen her somewhere before, but she seemed out of place now. From another town. Or from another era. She was wearing black engineers' boots with silver buckles and tight jeans and a black biker jacket over a tank top. She was smoking a cigarette. I was shoving some of the green UMass Lowell add-drop slips into my back pocket with my free hand. She was carrying two books. Maybe she was a student. Yes. I was sure I'd seen her before. Hanging out with the English-major types in the cafeteria last spring. But something was different now. She walked in a way that made the world wobble dangerously. It being autumn, I ascribed to her all the beauty of autumn. All the beauty, spread out across the entire United States of America. Rules of etiquette did not apply. I couldn't take my eyes off her. Nothing applied. Her path, once she became aware that I was heading her way, didn't deviate. Her eyes didn't waver.

"Hi," I said when we got close enough.

"Hi," she said.

We both stopped walking. She stood too close. We didn't smile. Something had already changed in us. Like the change of season. Or rain to snow. Falling faintly through the universe and faintly falling like the descent of . . . I don't know what.

But this is mostly bullshit. The truth is, I knew very well where I had seen her before. And I first fell in love with Deb during a late-night jerk-off session sometime during my 1989 spring semester. I had put a Betty Carter album on the turntable for ambience and was imagining all the girls in my Selected Authors class naked. There was a redheaded girl who was appealingly overweight. Then there was Lisa, the beautiful but uptight African-American girl who always wore owl glasses and dressed like a legal assistant. And then there was the older Italian woman who wore a wedding ring. And then there was the shy girl who sat next to the older Italian woman. The one who blushed whenever the professor asked her a direct question. The one who always wore those tight, sleeveless shirts. I didn't know her name at the time, but it was Deb. I imagined her to be a good girl. A pure girl. The sort of girl you should feel guilty about if you were to imagine her naked.

It helped that she was pretty. She's still pretty. Too pretty for me. I can tell when I look at the photographs of the two of us side by side. Don Hosier down at the supply house says I married over my head. Lots of guys make comments like this. I guess the broken-bridge look of my nose doesn't match the ruler-straight look of hers. And the droopy shape of my eyes doesn't match the crescent-moon shape of hers. People don't seem to enjoy my company the way they enjoy Deb's. She has a way of setting people at ease. It's partly her face that does it. Her eyes, unlike mine, take the shape of being very interested in whatever you might be saying, even if what you're saying is uninteresting. They frown at the serious parts and smile at the parts you intended to be funny. This trick makes you believe that she understands *exactly what you mean.* When the conversation is over, you walk away with the impression that she enjoys your company more than anyone else's in the world. She has a face that wouldn't say no. And I'm sure that, had I asked her in the proper way, in the will-you-marry-me way, she wouldn't have refused me. But I never did ask that way.

We had been dating for two months when we realized that we would be getting married. It was raining, and we were sitting in the cab of my gray Ford F-150 pickup truck. The windows were fogged up because my truck didn't have air-conditioning. "So," I said. Deb nodded, her eyes engaging mine the way they did. We both knew that she would soon be climbing out of the truck and dashing across the black, cold street and running up the two flights of stairs to the tenement apartment she shared with three other women. She would shower. And then she would dress in her

Ground Round uniform. And she would drive her car, a little Toyota Celica with a bad clutch, to work. "So," I said again. I didn't want her to go. She didn't want to go either. I could tell by her eyes. "I guess we're going to get married." She nodded again, her eyes narrowing. She understood exactly what I meant. "Yes," she said. "I think we are."

We were never ones for big decisions. Even marriage wasn't a decision we felt qualified to make. Marriage was, like everything else in our lives, just a thing that happened to us. An inevitable thing that overtook us. Like aging. Or fog on the windows. It's not that we didn't love each other. We did. We couldn't get enough of each other. We wanted to be together at all times. On Sundays we wanted to attend the Sergio Leone double feature at the Brattle Theatre in Harvard Square. After class, we wanted to sit together in the stairwells of 1950s brick buildings on the U Lowell campus and look out at the black, rain-soaked trees. We wanted to fish for carp together from the gravel parking lots on the Merrimack River, the rain dimpling the surface of the water. We wanted to eat teriyaki steak-and-cheeses together at Lena's over on North Campus. We wanted to sleep together, either in her freezing cold tenement or in my tiny, stiflingly hot, rent-controlled apartment in Cambridge. We wanted to eat chowder together at the Grog in Newburyport, then go out in the cold wind and swing on the swing set. Deb would scoot over and sit right next to me on the bench seat of the F-150. We'd drive to the county fair in Topsfield. Or to the mountains. Or to New Orleans. And everything just happened. Nothing we could do about it other than go out and buy a couple of gold rings. "Do you want an inscription?" asked the jeweler. "We can inscribe something inside if you like. The date maybe? Or maybe a line of poetry?"

"I'd like *Deb* in mine," I said. "What do you want in yours?"

"How about *Joe?*" she said.

Joe Blair

It was that simple. Inevitable. That we should have each other's names inscribed on the insides of our wedding rings. The jeweler, seeing how pleased we were with ourselves, rolled his eyes. "If you come up with anything good," he said, "let me know. We can always add it later."

By then, I had begun to rebuild the old KZ1000 and in the interim, in a mad fit of showroom passion, mortgaged my future on a new Honda ST1100, a sleek, fast, sport-touring machine that sort of looked like the Batmobile. The morning Deb and I left Massachusetts in the late summer of 1991, a few months after our elopement, the sky was clear and the air was cool. The black seat of the ST1100 was beaded with dew. I borrowed a bath towel from my parents to dry it off. (We had spent the night at my parents' house because we had already quit our jobs and let the rent-controlled place in Cambridge go.) The bike didn't start easily the way the KZ always did. It hesitated and then clattered to life, expelling white smoke from the exhaust pipes. I had spent days loading our gear. I fabricated a luggage rack and backrest out of rolled steel and pine slats. I strapped the tent sideways across the homemade rack and mounted the sleeping bags and pads on top of the fiberglass saddlebags like jet engines.

This was to be the beginning of the first real journey of our lives together. We weren't sure where we were going. We weren't sure whether or not we would return to Massachusetts. All we knew was that we had a motorcycle. And a tent. Two sleeping bags. Two leather coats and two pairs of chaps. Rain gear. Long underwear. Helmets. A few books. Jeans. Boots. Maps. And seven thousand dollars cleverly hidden in a white gym sock. These were the possessions that separated us from destitution.

The ST1100 clunked between gears. As I pulled onto Route 495. With my new bride on the back. Leaning on the sissy bar I had constructed. Her hands unzipping the pockets of my black leather jacket and tucking themselves inside. The drops of dew on the tank drawing themselves into retreating lines. Third gear. Fourth. (Clunk.) Fifth. Away from Billman's orchard. Away from Littleton. And Chelmsford. And Lowell and all the towns that had huddled around me for as long as I could remember, close and giant family members. Away from them. And Local Union 537, where I had completed my apprenticeship in the refrigeration trade. And my father, who waited until we were out of sight before he stopped waving.

Deb wore her hair in a single, thick braid that she tucked inside her leather jacket. I could feel her sigh. She was leaving too. Leaving was one major reason we got married. I wanted to leave. And she wanted to leave. We wanted to leave together. I didn't want to be the old guy in the Boston bar who sighs heavily and says, "I always wanted to leave." Little did I know I'd become the old guy in the Iowa City bar who sighs heavily and says, "I don't know why the hell I ever left!" We made our way northward, into the dense tangle of woods of eastern Massachusetts and Vermont and Quebec.

We didn't know it then, but we were young. We had thick hair. And lots of hope. When you're young and full of hope, you think that your leaving home constitutes a coming-of-age, a story that hinges on a character who starts out as a child, and through some series of events becomes a real live grown-up. It's a common blueprint. The protagonist is young. Full of wonder and earnestness and lust and anger. And he descends somehow. Falls. Or is thrown out. Either way, he leaves the garden behind.

Joe Blair

Deb and I ran out of money in Iowa. "We have one thousand left," said Deb, folding the bills and shoving them back inside the white gym sock. We were in a tent on the shore of Lake Macbride in Solon, Iowa, and it was raining as hard as I had ever seen it rain. In the Northeast, you get storms whipping up the coast that have names. Rachel. Agnes. Bob. And you get excited and drive to the ocean so you can see the big waves come crashing against the rocks. But hurricanes in the Northeast always disappoint. When you're a kid and you don't have anything to lose, you always want hurricanes to be bigger and more destructive than they turn out to be. All you end up with is a few plate-glass windows that have been blown out and a few old toolsheds that have collapsed. Iowa thunderstorms, on the other hand, don't disappoint. Midnight black clouds that spawn dozens of tornadoes, like wicked little devil children. Straight-line winds of up to one hundred miles per hour. When you hear the sirens, it doesn't mean you should jump in your car and drive somewhere so you can be entertained by the storm. It means, "Build an ark, motherfucker! Because God is pissed off!" The flash and crack of the storm was exploding all around our little brown Coleman tent. I was afraid. I looked at Deb, her features lit every so often by the strobe lightning that kept on coming. "What?" I said.

"One thousand," she shouted.

"What?" I shouted. We were inches apart, but the sound of the rain against the tent, mixed with the thunder, was deafening.

"You heard me!"

"Jesus Christ!" I shouted. "Where did it all go?" I felt like Captain America must have felt in *Easy Rider* when he said, "We blew it, man."

"Canada was pretty expensive!" she shouted.

"Last time, I made it to California and back on fifteen hundred."

"Not this time," she shouted.

That same week, we rented a small brick house seven miles west of Iowa City on what locals call the "Old IWV," which was the main highway from Iowa City to Des Moines before I-80 came through in the mid-1950s. The house we rented was one of three, sitting all in a row up on the ridge of a gentle swell in the land. The three brick houses were built for the three shift workers who spent their days and nights attending to what was, at one time, an oil line pumping station. The pumping station had been removed, but the houses were still there, wedged between a hog-farrowing pen and the Old Style beer distribution warehouse. There was a small bunch of buildings about a mile to the south and west that maps designated as a "town." A Catholic church and an old schoolhouse and a few houses. The school had been converted to a community center, where middle-aged guys played pickup basketball on weekends. But these details didn't interest us. We believed that we were only stopping in Iowa for a brief spell. Until we built up our war chest once again. For now, however, the little brick house would serve as our temporary home. We would pretend to be country folk—out with the pigs and corn and stuff. All the motion would stop for a while. A solitary meadowlark always returned to the phone line that ran in from the highway. I had never seen or heard one before and I fell in love with it, declaring the meadowlark my new favorite bird. I built flower boxes for the two front windows because Deb wanted them. She had this vision of what a "home" was supposed to look like. In the fall, we bought our first pumpkin, carved it up, put a candle inside it, and placed it beside the front door on Halloween night. We even bought a bag of "fun-size" Snickers bars, but we were in the country and no kids came.

Across the street, long after the corn had been harvested, cows would wander around silently in that gray light of winter, and we'd watch them

Joe Blair

from the front stoop. Deb and I both got jobs at a hardware store in the town of Oxford. It was owned by Al and Mary Wyborny, a handsome couple somewhere in their mid-sixties. I helped Al with water heater replacements and faucet repairs while Deb worked in the century-old store on Main Street with Mary. Mary taught Deb the difference between hex bolts and carriage bolts and lag bolts and toggle bolts and she instructed her to dust the lamps and small kitchen appliances and fans and little porcelain angels and kitty cats that cluttered the shelves. We were trying to behave the way we imagined married people were supposed to behave. We were doing our best, but even when Deb announced, one very cold day in January, that she was pregnant, it felt less like we were living the moment than like we were watching it on TV. The mother-to-be learns to cook casseroles. The father-to-be quits his job at the hardware store and goes back to the heating and air-conditioning trade in the hardworking, blue-collar city of Cedar Rapids. He dresses in his winter Carhartts and kisses his wife in the morning, leaving with a bag lunch—loving, handwritten note tucked inside—and returns again past dark to the delicious odor of some hamburger-based casserole bubbling in the oven. We painted the baby's bedroom a duckling yellow. In the spring, Deb planted multicolored pansies in the flower boxes I had built and all along the front walk. We bought a nice baby crib. Not the cheaper one, but the more expensive one, which, we quickly learned, did not include a mattress. So, of course we bought one of those too. And a fringe and comforter set with apples and balls and cats and all the letters of the alphabet. The comforter was small and much too stiff to conform to any shape, let alone the shape of a baby. But it didn't matter. There was a certain color in it that matched the curtains and Deb wanted it. So we bought it. Midsummer, we discovered the joy of fresh sweet corn sold by farmers' daughters who set up folding chairs behind their fathers' pickup trucks in gas station parking lots. We bought the mandatory plastic mobile that clips to the side of the crib and plays music when you turn the crank. Our big treat was waking up early and eating breakfast together at the sale barn in Oxford where the farmers auctioned off their cattle and hogs. There was no menu because the sale barn only offered one breakfast—two eggs with yolks a mustard orange, fresh bacon, and wheat toast. We bought a rocking chair we couldn't afford, but which Deb insisted upon because she imagined herself sitting in that particular rocking chair while she breast-fed our first child. By September, we thought we were ready. We figured we had done everything correctly. All the preparation we had done. All the waiting. And pretending.

S AM WAS BORN IN September of 1992.
William was born in June of 1994.
Lucy was born in January of 1998.

Deb wrote this information in the spaces provided on the inside flap of her Bible. They're simple facts, requiring no foresight at all.

What might it have meant for us if we could have had some foresight when it came to Lucy's twin brother, Michael? What if there existed, on the outskirts of town, when he was first born, an oracle? And we were to have brought the oracle a few gifts—a ring, a tripod, ten goats— and asked about our newborn child, and the oracle, after ruminating on the Truth of things, were to have opened her mouth and chanted, in the same annoying, singsong way Allen Ginsberg read his own poetry, the following:

Your son will be outcast from the gatherings of man. His language will be the language of the crows. Nor will any man understand his words nor will he understand the words of any man nor the crows. The residence of his soul will be the breeding place of flies, and he will be an abomination in the sight of men. He will walk in constant isolation all the days of his life. Thus the gods have blessed you with a great blessing; you have given birth to your own savior.

I'm sure we would have wanted the ring back. And the goats. She could keep the tripod because no one uses tripods anymore. As has always been the case with oracles and soothsayers and shamans and high priestesses of the apocalypse and other prophets, we would have come in faith and left in doubt and confusion. The language of crows? Our own savior? What could this mean?

In fact, we were told pretty much what my imaginary oracle told us by the neurologist at the University of Iowa Hospitals and Clinics (other than the part about giving birth to our own savior) ten years ago, five months before Michael was born. The neurologist gave us numbers. There was a statistical chance that our son would suffer from some degree of mental retardation and/or autism. In other words, there was a chance that he would be outcast from the gatherings of man etc. etc. etc..

When you ask about a condition, a doctor will, if she is able, give you a diagnosis based both on what she has observed in your particular case and the precedents recorded in history. These are the empirical results. When you ask about the future, a doctor will give you statistics. Five months before Mike was born, Deb and I were given statistics about our son's chances of having tuberous sclerosis, the disease he was eventually diagnosed with. The chances, we were told, were high. We were then given statistics about how affected he might be by the disease. He had a certain chance of being affected not at all. And a certain chance of being mildly affected. And a certain chance of being severely and profoundly affected. We took some comfort in knowing the name of our son's probable condition. And we took comfort in the statistical odds. But neither of these things have affected our son's condition in the least. Mike has almost no language. He has batches of seizures every two weeks or so now. This will change. They'll increase in frequency or decrease. They'll be more severe or less. Mike will be unable to sleep for days on end. Or he will sleep for days on end. No one knows why.

It's hard to argue with a diagnosis. The truth, after all, is the truth. An apple, for example, is an apple. There are no odds involved and it doesn't matter what you might believe it to be. You might believe it's a peach. You might believe it's a dirigible. It doesn't affect the apple in the least what you might believe. It's still an apple. It exists. And it is what it is.

Tuberous sclerosis, likewise, exists. It is what it is.

The above two sentences were very easy to write. And they can be nothing but true. There is no argument that would convince anyone otherwise.

Mike exists. And he is who he is.

But who he will be cannot be quantified by numbers. The future is up for grabs. And what we believe in; what we pray for; what we hope for has the power to change it.

Joe Blair

I believe a lot of things. I could write one of those self-important essays for NPR about what I believe. I believe, for example, that my son, Mike, understands much more than he lets on. I believe he understands exactly what I'm saying when I talk to him. And I believe he has an idea of who he is and how he is perceived in the world as much as any of us do. I believe he suffers because of his limitations. I believe his feelings are hurt when he gets shouted at for doing things he can't help but do. I believe he is afraid at times. And happy at times. And I believe he is capable of love. I have faith that these things are true. In other words, I believe them to be true. Proof not withstanding. This is how love works. It's belief that brings love into being. As if from thin air. Belief. An ethereal notion. An idea that has the power to create and destroy. We need it, this belief. This prayer. This hope. So that, in time, when the future is worn away by the present, the past might show that we have held up some kind of light, however dim, in the surrounding darkness of the world.

Deb still tells me she loves me. In all the time I've known her, she has repeated this sentiment. We don't talk much about our future plans anymore because Mike has canceled most of them out. "We should go to France!" I might say. But we both know that's not going to happen. How will we deal with Mike? He shouts and squeals so loudly most of the time, we can't stay in a hotel. Will we be able to find French fries in France? If there are no French fries in France, what will Michael eat? He doesn't seem to like anything else. "We should go to a movie!" "We should go to a museum!" "We should go camping!" None of these things, we have discovered through trial-and-error, are good ideas for family activities. So, we don't talk about the future much anymore. Other than whether or not we've picked up the prescription at Walgreens. Or when I'll be home from work. We don't talk about much involving what you might call "love" either. But still, every time we finish a phone conversation Deb says, "Bye. I love you." And I respond, "Bye. I love you too." This exchange is sort of like a woman who, while running her electric hedge-trimmers, shouts to you over the noise, explaining that what she's doing is, in fact, washing her car. It just doesn't make sense. But here's the thing: If a woman explains this same thing to you every day for sixteen years, shouting over the noise of her electric hedge-trimmers, explaining to you that she's washing her car, you might convince yourself that it's only natural to wash your car this way, by passing this noisy electric device back and forth over the hedgerow until it's all square and unnatural looking. This is what washing your car looks like.

A few things have changed since the time when Deb and I dressed in black leather and rode the motorcycle every day and pissed, from a great height, on all the quaint little towns we passed through. Now we live in one of those quaint little towns. On the road, we would laugh at the quirky people who sold things at quirky garage sales. New we're affixing masking tape to the old waffle iron, conferring about the price. "How much for the waffle iron? Five bucks?" On the road, I wore my Ray-Bans. Now I wear the plastic knockoffs my daughter found on the street. The bikes are long gone. We sold them a few months after William was born—the ST1100 to some BMW nerd from Strawberry Point who was shocked that I didn't wear ear protection when I rode and then angry to find out I had modified the original tool kit that came with the bike. And my fabled KZ1000 to a kid from Oxford who bought it, he said, for parts. It broke my heart to sell a thing I owned as completely as anyone can own a thing.

Dust to dust.

We got enough out of the bikes for the down payment on our first family car. When I told the guy at the used car dealership we had two kids and two on the way, he leaned close and informed me that, in his professional opinion, we had fucked ourselves into a minivan.

We tend to forget, after so many years in Iowa, how beautiful it is. We go about our little Iowa City routines, driving the same routes that, when you add them up, total twenty-two thousand, three hundred miles a year. Deb knows this because she did the math when we traded the old Honda Odyssey for the new Honda Odyssey. I wonder if it bothers her how many miles she has driven and still she hasn't gotten anywhere. If only she took those miles and drove new highways. She would have covered most of North and South America by now. She could have seen the Mayan ruins and the Grand Tetons and Lake Powell. Dipped her toe in the waters off Cape Horn. But she hasn't been anywhere. She retraces the same routes just like I do. Iowa City to Cedar Rapids. River Street to West Music in Coralville. River Street to the Hy-Vee supermarket on Riverside. These are the points of interest on our travelogue.

We own an actual house now, a century-old, two-story place in an old neighborhood with huge, gnarly bur oaks all around. Our actual house has an actual driveway that needs to be shoveled on occasion and an actual yard that needs to be mowed. Since we were married, we have aged about sixteen years. Just like everyone else.

THE WIND MOVES WITH a purpose. Nothing is in its proper place. Everything needs to be rearranged. Home from the Luther College science building, I notice that the trash barrel I left at the curb this morning is lying in the street. Recyclable materials fly past the old windows of our pale yellow house on the corner of River and Woolf—Iowa City, Iowa. Pine boughs lash the air like angry things.

"We should go," I tell Deb, as I kick off my work boots by the garage door and turn to hang my blue hoodie on the coatrack. "We could just . . . go. What do you think? Just move somewhere else. What do you think? Just . . . go."

"Do you think," Deb says, after a long pause, "that we should paint Lucy's bedroom pearl or a colder white?" She says she doesn't want it *too* white, because that will look *awful*.

Deb and I are about to be engaged in what has been the defining argument of our marriage. We know it by heart. Like the black-and-white nuns from the Franco American School in Lowell know the rosary, all those old women clogging the benches along the Merrimack River, clutching their beads and repeating the same words over and over. I say, "I think we should go back to New England." Then I tell her why. I tell her that the hills and the trees and the water and the rock walls and the heavy snow and short, flaming summers make me feel more alive. "I know it's expensive," I say, "but we can do it. I can support us. I'll be happier there. And I think you've forgotten what it's like. We could go to the ocean. And the pizza's better. I think you'll be happier, too."

Deb is silent for a long time. She frowns. She acts as though she were thinking about what I've just said. She's not. She knew what I'd say before I said it just like I know what she'll say next. What she's considering now is how long to wait before saying, "You'll be miserable there just like you're miserable here. It's just more of the same."

"But—" I say.

"I'm just not excited about moving there and having you fix air conditioners," she says. "It's the same thing as here."

"Well, if it's the same—"

"That's my point," she says. "It's the same. You'll still be fixing air . . ."

And we argue.

I tell her to forget about what she thinks *I* might want. "What about *you?*" I say. "How do *you* feel about it? Forget about me and the kids!"

She won't forget about the kids. She can't. She talks about Michael, our severely and profoundly autistic son. "It exhausts me to think I'll have to start all over again with Michael," she says. "We get thirty hours of respite a month here," she says. "And music therapy, and occupational therapy, and ..." There are five or six therapies. I can't remember them all.

Deb is a paramedic. She works in the ER when she's not in the truck. She likes the calls where she can make a difference, especially diabetic emergency calls, "because I can fix them up so quickly," she says. "Just give them an infusion of D50, and they're good as new. It's like a miracle." But more often she ends up taxiing drug seekers to the hospital or triaging psych patients who spend their time inventing symptoms. One time, a young woman dialed 911 because she had menstrual cramps. "And we had to take her in," Deb said. "It's protocol." She hates those frivolous calls. The drug seekers who describe phantom pains in order to attain their drug of choice, Dilaudid or hydrocodone or some other narcotic. She hates frivolous things altogether.

I tell Deb I'll do the research. I'll find out what's available for Michael in Massachusetts. Then she repeats her argument once again. She says she won't move to the coast if I'm fixing air conditioners. That's just doing the same thing. She'll only move to the coast if I'm a writer or a teacher. Only if I'm a writer or a teacher and only if we can live right on the ocean. Right on it. "So we can hear the waves at night," she says.

"Sure," I say. "We'll live on the ocean. And I'll write. And we won't have to worry about the mortgage. Because the monkeys will take care of that."

"Monkeys?" says Deb. "What monkeys?"

I cross my arms. "You know what monkeys," I say.

Deb crosses her arms and frowns.

"If I start my own business *out there*," I say, "we'll be able to afford—"

41

"You have your own business *here*," she says.

This conversation is driving me crazy. It never varies.

"Yeah," I say. "I know it. But *I hate Iowa*."

"You hate everything," she says calmly.

"Yeah," I say, "well, you . . ." I can't think of anything zippy to say.

"Think about someone other than yourself," she says, after a pause. "The kids are all doing so well! Mike is doing pretty well, and Lucy has finally made some friends, and Sam's got debate, and William is going to be in that play. He's so excited. And I think this might be the thing for him. I can't understand why you'd want to leave!"

I call her selfish for not caring whether or not I'm happy.

She tells me I don't know what love is. "It's not about you," she says. She calls me selfish for even thinking of breaking up the great hand she believes we've been dealt, and I know she's right. It's not a bad hand. Who could complain? I don't know why I argue. I don't want to argue. I want to make Deb happy. I always have. Not so much out of love. But because when she's happy, she's not accusing me of anything. And I'm much more likely to make Deb happy if I agree with her rather than disagree. If I agree that, yes, we should stay in Iowa forever. And, yes, we should buy a puppy for the kids, even though I never really wanted a puppy. And, yes yes yes . . .

I named the dog, but Deb named all four of the kids. I'm not blaming her. I ceded this power to her and I have never complained about having no say in the naming of our children because, after all, I never went through the pain of childbirth. It's not that I didn't care or have an opinion. I wanted Sam to be Henry. I wanted William to be Calvin. I wanted Lucy to be Scarlett. I wanted Michael to be Gabriel. And I wanted Deb to be happy. And I told myself that names, after all, are only words. Tags for much more substantial things. And once the tags are in place, all you need to do is accept them.

Sure, I argue about moving away. But I'm not sure I even *want* to move back to New England. I'm sort of frightened when I consider actually doing it—giving everything up. I'm just arguing now. Just saying things. I don't even mean them. I get sleepy. Very, very sleepy. I can't talk anymore. My eyes have lost all lubrication. They're full of sand. I walk to the bedroom. I can still hear Deb talking. I can't hear exactly what she's saying. It's something about something and something else. I'm not sure. I fall on the bed, disgusted with myself. The wind pushes against the old windows. I think it would like nothing better than to shatter them.

IN THE LIVING ROOM is a leather couch and a fireplace and a floor lamp with one of those three-in-one lightbulbs that is good for reading. It's midmorning on a Saturday in late May and I am reading aloud to my ten-year-old daughter, Lucy. I have a hot cup of tea balanced on the arm of the couch. A three-dollar Duraflame log is burning in the fireplace. The ongoing sound of rain overflowing the gutters. A noise from the kitchen: something clanking against something else. A metallic noise. I try to ignore it because I'm comfortable and I don't want to get up. Lucy is staring at the unnaturally blue and yellow flames, waiting for me to continue.

" 'Seven days since your last battle, Ender,' said Graff. Ender did not reply."

The metallic clanking grows louder.

"Shit," I say, springing to my feet.

"Dad!" says Lucy, shocked.

"Sorry, honey," I say. "I'll be right—" I'm moving toward the swinging door between the stairway and the kitchen. We need to keep the doors shut because we've decided to keep d'Artagnan restricted to the kitchen. D'Artagnan is our dog. He likes to piss on the rug in Michael's bedroom. As I swing the door open, being careful not to let him through, I see that Michael is spooning the chili that has been simmering on the stovetop onto the floor. "Michael!" I shout. "Get away from there! That's hot!" I grab the spoon from him. He begins to cry. "No!" I say. "That's hot! That will burn you!" Now Michael is crying very loudly. "What's wrong?" I say. "Use your words. Daddy . . ." I begin his sentence for him. "Daddy, I want . . . Say it, Michael. Daddy. I want . . ." Michael is screaming at the top of his lungs now. The dog is very excited by the screaming. He is leaping up on Michael. Michael pushes the dog away. "Okay, Michael," I say. "You've got to get out of the kitchen. Stay away from the stove. That's hot." Michael continues to cry.

The term *mental retardation* is used less and less now. For a while, everyone used the term *mentally challenged*. But that too seems to have gone by the wayside. The terms have short shelf lives, probably because they quickly work their way into our everyday vocabulary in the form of insults. A century ago, when neurologists were first learning how to diagnose tuberous sclerosis, the term used was *idiocy*. The word *idiot* comes from the Greek. It means "private." Michael is very private. He seems to be all alone in the world. He lives in a place that makes him suddenly scream at the top of his lungs. And then, just as suddenly, laugh hysterically. Michael flies into rages for reasons hidden from us. And he breaks things. Lamps. Toys. He punches out windows. At ten years old, Michael already weighs over a hundred pounds. He's off the charts in the height department too. He's going to be a very big man. Once his body begins to go through the changes of puberty, they say the frequency of his erratic behavior will probably increase. No big surprise there. Already, one of his favorite hobbies is playing with his penis. A chip off the old block in that department. When he discovers orgasm, I'm sure he'll never give his penis a moment's rest. But his life has not yet been corrupted by orgasm. He's only ten. He likes to take baths. He likes to sing along with songs he knows. And he likes to wrestle. He's always smiling when I wrestle with him. It's getting harder to wrestle him gently to the ground now that he's gotten so big and strong, and of course he'll only get bigger and stronger even as Deb and I get smaller and weaker. When the day comes that he can overpower us, that will be the day we'll be in trouble. Because when Michael realizes that he can do what he wants, no one knows exactly what he will do.

Michael pees in return air registers. He laughs and laughs and laughs and laughs. He laughs for hours. Sometimes, he laughs through the night. Some guys start research centers to find a cure for whatever might be ailing their child. I haven't started any research centers. I don't know how anyone with a kid like Michael has time to start a research center. When I'm home, I don't do much of anything except clean up after him. I also seem to find the time to be angry with him and with whatever fate or divine power or circumstance that has twisted his path around mine. I used to spank his bottom. I thought this was the way fathers were supposed to behave. But the spankings didn't do any good. Not for him and not for me. It would happen like this: Maybe Michael would take a shit in the bathtub again and I'd only notice as I reached in the water to wash him. There'd be dark shapes lurking in the bottom of the tub like brown trout. "Unbelievable!" I'd shout. "Mike! Why do you do that?" I'd pull him out of the tub and dry him and drain the water and scoop the brown trout into the toilet with a handful of wadded-up toilet paper. Then I'd clean the tub with Lysol and then I'd fill the tub again and then I'd come downstairs to find Michael naked, finishing up a package of raw pork sausage he'd stolen from the fridge. Then I might swat his butt. It would take a few moments before he'd cry. And when he did cry, it would be the cry of the unjustly accused. He hadn't intended to displease his father. What had he done that was so bad? He had only pooped because he had to poop, just like everyone else, and then he had eaten because he was hungry, just like everyone else. What was so bad? When Michael would cry, I'd realize what a schmuck I had been, spanking my autistic son for doing something he didn't know was wrong.

Sometimes I get the sense, when Michael looks at me with that distant stare, that he's not really looking at me at all, rather beyond me into some other place where everything makes some other sense. Strange that a child who has such interruptions in his brain, such irregular electrical impulses—a child who suffers from seizures, who shouts out as if in either pain or an overflow of exuberance—would possess at times such a crystalline calm about him. Sometimes, when we're all alone and he looks beyond me the way he does into that world of other-sense, I get the unsettling feeling that I am looking into the face of God.

Every word I say to Michael might be said in absolute isolation. Or, it might echo in eternity. The endless refrain of what I know is right and what I know is wrong. There is no one to tell me whether I have spanked my son's bottom justly or unjustly. But Michael will look beyond me the way he does, and I'm tempted to turn around and see who, exactly, he's looking at and whether or not someone is angry with *me*.

We have a school picture of Michael stuck to the fridge. There he is: looking beyond us in that way autistic kids do. It's not a look distinct to Michael. There are medical reasons for it I'm sure. Most people might find the look on Michael's face slightly disturbing. They'd use the word *vacant* to describe it. I study Michael's face now as it appears in his school picture. There is not a line in it. And, apart from the eyes, it is the face of a sleeping boy. There is no forced smile. No glimmer of impatience or anxiety. There is nothing but peace.

I don't spank him anymore. There's something about hitting a person who has so much trouble with communication that is certainly wrong. After I'd spank him, I'd be aware that I had failed a test. Without anyone looking. Without anyone ever knowing about it. I had been tested and I had failed. I always felt bad. Not ten minutes would go by before I'd be hugging him and telling him I was sorry. I'd tell him I loved him. I'd tell him I was proud of him. It would be an absurd thing to observe if anyone were indeed observing me. *Here. Look at this odd behavior! A man shouts and hits a child for eating raw pork; then the man hugs the child and tells the child he's proud of him. Why is the man doing these things?* Michael always seemed to forgive me. When I hugged him, he always hugged me back and kissed me on the cheek in his too-wet, too-hard way. And then I knew that there was something great and slow moving beyond me. Another world I was not privy to. A world with a boy in it. No more innocent a boy in this world. No boy who deserved a spanking less. No boy with a face so completely without artifice.

I push Michael toward the other swinging door, which opens onto the dining room. "Stay out of the kitchen," I say. I grab a dirty hand towel and wet it in the sink. Then I kneel in front of the stove and begin to clean up the mess.

Back on the couch.

"Let's see . . . where were we?"

Lucy leans against me.

"'Seven days since your last battle,'" I read.

"You read that," says Lucy.

"'Ender did not reply . . .'"

The clanking sound again.

"Michael!" I shout. "Get away from that stove!"

The clanking stops.

I pause, ready to jump up again. But the kitchen remains silent.

"Okay," I say. "Let's see . . ."

"'Ender did not reply.'"

D'Artagnan skids around the corner from the dining room into the living room. He regains his balance and starts leaping toward Lucy and me, ears flapping wildly. I spring up again and run toward the kitchen. Michael has managed to dish some chili onto an enormous serving plate (the one we use for turkey on Thanksgiving), which he balances on the edge of the stove. "No, Michael!" I shout. I gently take the spoon away from him, afraid he might suddenly decide to fling some boiling hot chili from the pot into the air, but he doesn't fling. He just looks at me sadly. "Okay, Michael," I say. "I know you're hungry." I continue dishing chili from the pot onto the large serving platter. Michael looks hopeful. "Okay," I say, turning toward the fridge. "Let's put an ice cube in here. You like ice cubes." I reach into the freezer and pry two ice cubes free from one of the trays. I stir in the ice cubes with my finger. "There," I say, turning and placing the platter on the kitchen table. I cross the room for a fork. By the time I'm back to the table, Michael is gone.

"'Seven days since your last battle, Ender,' said Graff."

"'Ender did not reply.'"

There is a loud clattering sound. I jump up from the couch again and sprint to the kitchen. D'Artagnan has leapt onto the kitchen table and knocked the chili onto the floor, shattering the platter.

The puppy DVD says you should never give the dog negative reinforcement. No loud voices. No punishments. Everything should be treats and kindness. The same way we're supposed to raise our kids. And follow God's Word. What word that might be I can't tell you exactly. But they say there is a word. Somewhere. And I'm sure there's a lot to be said for the joy of "letting go and letting God." And I understand that people need to get used to the idea of "giving it up" as they say, but here's the thing: As far as I know, Jesus was a bachelor. He never had any kids. (Or pets either, for that matter.) And here's what seems to be missing from all of these ideas of "joy" and "letting go": Someone has to train the dog.

I grab the dog by the collar. "No!" I say in an angry voice. The puppy looks frightened. "No!" I say again, while hustling him out the door and into the rain. He, like Michael, has no idea what he's done wrong. What has he done wrong? Isn't he supposed to lick up stuff when it spills on the floor? Isn't he supposed to be full of energy? I wet down the hand towel again and begin to clean up the mess. With as much joy in my heart as I can muster. Michael swings open the door from the dining room. "Michael," I say in a strong voice. He wants to walk through the broken glass and spilled chili. There is nothing he wants more. He leans toward it. "Michael," I say in the voice of the Old Testament God, "do not come in here!" Michael lets the door swing closed and disappears.

Joe Blair

My tea is cold.

"'Seven days since your last battle, Ender,'" said Graff.

"What took you so long, Dad?" says Lucy.

"'Ender did not reply.'"

"Dad, we already read this part."

IF THERE WERE SUCH a place as heaven, a place of absolute love and absolute peace, and in this heaven there were such beings as angels, beings beyond language and time, and one of these angels were to visit you at home, I'm sure it would be an uncomfortable affair. The angel might look right through you. Through you and beyond you. After all, the angel would be an absolute being. The angel might be prone to fits of absolute rapture or absolute agony depending on . . . what? You would have no way of knowing. I don't think an angel would take a shit in the bathtub. I don't think an angel would shit at all. Neither would he crack all twelve eggs on the countertop. Or repeatedly flood the backyard with water from the hose. But what do I know? Maybe angels do these things all the time.

Michael learns words and forgets them. When he was seven, he loved the words *rainbow* and *macaroni*, and he'd say them with enthusiasm, independently, apropos of nothing. Now he never says these words. They're gone. Between the ages of five and eight, he knew how to use the toilet. Now he's back in diapers. At one time he could say, "My name is Michael Blair." If you asked him where his nose was, he could point it out to you. No more. At the moment, Michael has no language. Other than the one sentence that has survived the years.

Joe Blair

Michael will scream so loudly it's unbearable. "Mike," Deb or I will say, "use your words. Use your words." And he'll always say the same thing. The only sentence that has never deserted him: "I want more please." That's what he says. He says the words with a slight pause after each one, as if each word had nothing to do with the preceding one. He says his sentence, and then he looks hopefully in our direction, if not into our eyes. "I want more please." "More what?" we say. "Mike. What do you want more of? What do you want?" He will be frustrated that we don't understand. And he will say again, more urgently this time but still in his halting, robotic way, "I want more please."

And the guessing game begins. "Do you want cereal?" we say, holding up the box of gluten-free corn puffs. "You want juice? Juice?" We hold up the juice. "You want a book?" "You want to go outside?" "You want a bath?" "You want your string?" "You want to go for a walk?" "You want an orange?"

Mike will storm and scream and stomp. Because we've got it wrong. We've got it all wrong. And then, when we tell him once again to use his words, he will calm himself and try one more time. "I want more please."

W HEN DEB FINISHES HER shift at St. Luke's, it is a great relief
and a bright light in the darkness for both of us to jump in my
truck and drive down to the Wig and Pen. There's a gas fireplace and an
old-fashioned-English-pub-type atmosphere, an atmosphere that is very
even and calm and if it could talk it would say, "There there. It's okay. It's
all right. I'll take care of you. Why don't you stay for a while? Yes. That's it.
Have a drink. There, now. Are you feeling better? Terrific. That's terrific.
Now, let me tell you something: You know all that bullshit out there? Out
those doors? That bathtub stuff? That raw sausage stuff? That pee in the
registers stuff? It's not real. No. No it's not, my little friend. No. All that
stuff? It's an *illusion*."

The Wig and Pen has become a part of our routine. We always order the
same thing. A pitcher of Bass. And I'll smoke one or two cigarettes (a
new habit for me). The nicotine goes to my head. The alcohol goes there
too. And I climb into my little airplane and take a test flight around and
around the ceiling of the pub, up where the smoke is, the smoke that
might be clouds, up there where the ceiling fan wheels slowly and silently
on its bearings.

"So," says Deb, when we're settled at the table near the fireplace, "I went through the Verizon bill today."

"Yeah?" I say. I'm not looking at her. I'm looking at the TV, which is mounted up high, in the corner behind the bar. It's Cubs baseball. Derrek Lee is up.

"Yeah. You have anything to say?"

"About what?"

"About who you've been calling."

"When?" I say.

"You know when," she says.

"No," I say, shifting my gaze to her and then back to the TV. "I don't. That's why I'm asking."

"That's bullshit!" she says. "You don't call someone ten times and—"

"Oh, Jesus!" I shout. "That fucking guy!"

"What guy?"

"Lee," I say, as Derrek Lee, strikeout victim, walks slowly back to the dugout.

When I was a kid, I watched this TV special about a guy who sailed around the world all by himself. And like every kid who watched that show, I thought, maybe someday I'll sail around the world all by myself too. I thought it was possible. Why not? Some might say the difference between being a kid and being a grown-up is that grown-ups don't think they can sail around the world all by themselves. Why not? Because they don't have a sailboat. Because they couldn't make the mortgage payments if they sailed around the world. Because they don't know how to sail. Because they don't want to. Because it's just a TV show. There can be a lot of becauses. There can be endless becauses. Because you're a grown-up. Because you have responsibilities. Because you haven't made one choice in the last ten years. Because (and here's the important one) you're a coward. Yes. That's right. Because you, my little friend, are a coward. When you're a kid, on the other hand, your entire thought process is consumed with visions of *what might be*. You are propelled forward in search of some foggy thing. Some thing that you believe might be amazing. What you might do. Who you might be. You imagine that there are so many possibilities.

I don't put sandwiches in the freezer for my lunch anymore like I did when I was a kid, thinking they'll keep just fine and taste great later in the week. And I don't so much chase the future as I try to avoid being caught by the misery my ex-future has turned out to be. Our history gains more weight day by day. There can be no denying this. And the future seems more and more unlikely to be anything cool at all. And my circumstances seem more and more difficult to change. I think it would take an act of great faith or courage to change my circumstances when my life is nothing but a repetition. And a repetition. And the more I repeat, the more afraid I become of change. The less able I am to believe I can have any effect on my own life. And yet, somehow, I'm always advising others to be brave and have the courage to change their circumstances. In fact, I'm the Pied Piper of what might be called freedom.

"You just need to get the hell out of here," I told Matt Strong last Monday night. I know it was Monday because Saul Uberoth was blowing his horn and they had the Hammond B3 set-up blocking the front entrance of George's Tap and that's what they do on Monday nights. They call it Blues Jam. Matt Strong was complaining. "I haven't been laid in six months," he said. Matt is not young, but he's handsome enough and has enough money to take vacations each year. Last year, for instance, he took a ski vacation to Colorado for two weeks. "You've got to get the hell out of Iowa," I advised him.

He squinted at me. "Why?" he said.

"I don't know," I said. "I just think you've been here too long. That's all."

"How is me moving out of Iowa going to help me get laid?" he said.

"I don't know," I said, taking another haul from my pint glass. The music was heating up and my friend Saul, the sax player, had already begun his inevitable stroll among the patrons, blowing his horn and making us all feel that we were somehow participating in the music. "Let's face it," I said, "and don't deny it: All the women around here know you too well." I looked toward Saul and then, after a beat or two, snuck a look at Matt. I laughed loudly at the expression on his face and he joined in laughing.

"Fuck you," he said. "And besides," he added, after Saul had made his way back up onto the stage, "I can't go anywhere. I'm stuck."

I turned until I was facing Matt straight on, very interested in why he might be stuck.

"Why do you say that?" I said.

"It's not like I've got a trade like you," he said. "I can't make thirty bucks an hour. I'm a housepainter for fuck sake. I go somewhere else and I'm making . . . what? Ten bucks an hour? But here, I've got a business. I charge fifty-five an hour. I've got clients lined up. And I do a perfect job. They know that. That's why they hire me."

"But your house is paid for," I said. "You could sell that or—"

Matt snorted loudly.

"—or rent it or whatever," I continued, "and that would be a thousand or two per month and you could—"

"Joe," said Matt, patting me on the chest, pushing me back into my stool. "Joe JoeJoeJoe. Calm yourself. Okay? Calm down. You don't know what you're talking about. Okay? I can't go. Can't!" Saying this, he held his hands up in the air like when the dove has just appeared behind the silk scarf. And voilà!

He can't go. And Deb can't go. And I can't go. Nobody can go.

Life can hypnotize you into thinking that you have no choice. That you're trapped. You have a mortgage. You have a job. You have a wife. You have children, one of whom will never dress himself. Never hold a conversation. Never fall in love. And you will provide. This will be your life. What choice do you have in the matter? Things will always be this way.

Enter the Wig and Pen. Whispering her lullabies. The Wig and Pen. My hope and my childhood. My future and my past.

It was only a few years ago when Deb and I spoke about the possibility of traveling to San Sebastián, Spain. Or spending a week in New York City. Or selling everything and buying a camper and traveling around the country. Maybe we could study the history of the various places we visited and the kids would learn so much more on the road rather than spending another year in school. And I could write and draw and Deb could write and sculpt and then, when our money was gone, we could get jobs somewhere and live in the trailer home. And why couldn't we do that? Why couldn't we? And then, thinking about these things, reclining in my booth at the Wig and Pen, I light a cigarette, and Deb comments on the way the lights look, amber and beautiful, when she views them through her full pint glass of Bass ale, and I exhale a plume of smoke, and we imagine things. We imagine things together, Deb and I.

This is why I want Deb to drink. It's not because I want to destroy her. It's because I want to be in love again. I want the two of us to be brave. And give everything away. And be iconoclastic. And idiosyncratic. And artistic. And I have discovered that we can be all of this without changing a single thing in our lives other than our sobriety.

So, we get drunk. And we get sober again. And the days go by. I know there must be more. This advance and retreat can't be all there is. Freezing and melting. Repair and disrepair. Sobriety and drunkenness. Sleep and wakefulness. The days go by. The silent water. But there must be more. There must be something absolute. There must be something that never changes. "Use your words," we say. "Use your words."

"It's all bullshit, though," sighs Deb.

"I know it," I say. "I know it." I breathe. I glance at the game and then at my wife. "Um," I say. "What?"

Deb leans forward, squinting. "I know," she says.

"You know what?" I say.

"I just know. That's all."

"You know what?"

"I know about *her*," she says.

I force a laugh. "Really?" I say. "*Her?* You do? You know about *her?*"

"Who do you call ten times in a day?" says Deb.

"I didn't call—"

"No," she says. "Not who *did* you call; who *do* you call. It's a hypothetical. Who do you call ten times in a day? Who do you call that often? Do you call anyone that often? A golf buddy? An auto mechanic? Who do you call ten times a day?"

"Okay," I say. "I give up. Who do you call ten times a day?"

"Me? I don't call anyone ten times a day."

"Jesus Christ," I say. "Is this, like, a comedy . . . thing . . . or something?"

"You don't call *me* ten times a day," she says, grabbing her pint glass. "I know that."

"If you're so curious," I say, "why don't you call the number?"

"I tried!" she shouts.

"Deb," I say. "Could you keep it down?"

"Keep it down?" she shouts, wild-eyed.

"I've got to pick William up," I say.

"Want to change the subject, huh?" she says.

"The phone calls?" I say, leaning close. "They're about rotisserie baseball. I didn't want to tell you because I know you don't want me doing that again this year."

Joe Blair

"Bullshit," she says.

"Here," I say, pulling out my phone. "I'll call Marty right now. You want to talk to him?"

"No."

"I'll get William," I say, standing and shoving my phone back into my pocket. "Hey, you know what? I'll walk over. You take the truck."

"But you just poured me another beer! How can I take the truck? Besides, have you looked outside lately?" She throws her chin in the direction of the window.

Rain. Of course.

If you take a right out of the parking lot of the Wig and Pen, and then a left on Mormon Trek past the softball complex where we play our league games, you'll hook up with Route 1 and be coasting through the rolling Iowa towns with bucolic names like Lone Tree and Richland and Fairfield. The road, I'm sure, doesn't care one way or the other if you drive away on it, and before long, if you take the proper turnoffs, you'll see signs for towns with names like St. Louis and then Atlanta and then Miami, where, if you wanted to, you could apply for a job.

If you turn around in the Hardee's parking lot, where a club called the Cruise-O-Matics has antique car shows every other Friday night in the summertime, you'll end up back on Route 80, which has no problem with you driving away on it either. Plenty of people have done it. You could drive straight to New York City and maybe rent a tiny apartment in the Bronx.

Of course, you can also just keep going straight if you want. That will bring you along the Coralville Strip. There's a bunch of stuff down there too.

Joe Blair

But I won't go any of these directions. I'll take a right on First Ave and then a left on Fifth Street. I'll pick up William from his kickboxing class and then, when I get to the intersection again, I'll take a left. Because that's where I live. My wife and I. And our four children. And our dog, d'Artagnan. And our lawn mower. And our snow shovels. And our high-speed Internet connection, which costs me almost a hundred bucks a month. And my bicycle, which I never ride. And my canoe, which never leaves the garage. That's where I'll be heading.

The cross traffic gets the green light and the cars move along.

Sometimes, Deb complains about picking up and dropping off the kids. But I sort of like it. I like it in the same way I like waiting for my clothes to dry at the Laundromat. Because there aren't really any decisions to make. You can't go walking out of the Laundromat for a half hour and try to accomplish something else while your clothes dry. I did that once at a Laundromat on Mass Ave in Cambridge and three pairs of my Levi's were gone when I got back. You need to wait. That's just the way it is.

With these things I repeat, like glancing at the red digits on the alarm clock before I switch off my reading light and roll over on my side and give myself up to sleep, it seems like the time between the last event and the current event is almost nonexistent. The thing happens and then it happens again and so on. This has been my life. So far. As far as I can tell, there haven't been any decisions to make. I pull up to the intersection and I pull up and I pull up and I pull up. And I'm always going somewhere. It's not like I pull up to the intersection and then decide where I'm going. I already know. It isn't so bad, really.

"You have a good practice?" I ask my fourteen-year-old son.

William shrugs.

"No?"

"Yeah," he says, looking away. "I guess."

A few months ago, when I pulled up to the intersection, it was snowing. The snowflakes were very large, having piggybacked on other snowflakes on the way down. Like little falling nuclear families of snowflakes. It was the very beginning of a squall and the air temperature was somewhere below zero. Still, the flakes were very large, which I remember thinking was strange, it being so cold. And I figured there must have been some temperature inversion a few thousand feet up. The intense yellow lights from the perimeter of the Hawkeye Softball Complex glanced off the black, oil-soaked patch of asphalt between the four sets of traffic lights. There were also some lights from the Walgreens on the opposite corner. I could see very clearly the snowflakes when they hit the road, drifting sideways on the wind and then shattering into tiny fragments. Skidding slightly. Taking their time to shatter. It fascinated me, for some reason, these snowflakes shattering against the cold surface. And the lights. It made me think of birds landing on water.

"You learn anything?" I ask my son.

William shrugs.

I nod.

When I get home, I'm thinking, I'll need to put Michael to bed. I know he won't stay in bed unless I get in bed with him. I'll tell him to get back into bed fifty times. "Michael," I'll say. "Get back in bed!" Fifty times. This may sound like an exaggeration to you, but it's a conservative estimate. And after the first thirty or so times, I'll need to work hard on staying calm. Shouting doesn't help. It only makes Michael cry and then I'll feel bad and comfort him and tuck him under his covers and then he'll stay there for thirty seconds and then he'll get out of bed. We never imagined, when we named him Michael, that we'd have to say it so many times. "Michael, get back in bed!" It's not that he doesn't listen. He listens. And he gets back in bed. And then, having gotten back in bed, he gets out of bed again. After I lie down with Michael for a while, I'll brush my teeth and then I'll climb into my bed. Before I turn over on my side, I'll glance at the clock.

At the intersection, I flip on the radio, expecting country or sports talk, but what comes through the speakers surprises me. It's Kathleen Battle, the prima donna who, as the story goes, while riding in a California limo, phoned her management company in New York to tell them she was too cold. The management company then called the limousine company in L.A., who contacted the chauffeur, who adjusted the set point on the air conditioner. I recognize the requiem mass by Gabriel Fauré. Actually, I know it quite well. But this particular version, so suddenly filling the car, unnerves me and shakes something loose that I thought was torqued down pretty well.

One time, I drove out to the Macbride Nature Recreation Area with Deb and the kids and the dog and we found a camping area overlooking the reservoir. The wind tore at us, but we didn't care because it was a warm wind, and we couldn't help but run. I ran and ran and so did Deb and all the kids and the dog at the time, Maggie, and we were down by the lake and then back up at the campsite and we had brought Sunkist orange soda at the little grocery store in North Liberty, and some chips, and six huge apples, and we had a little picnic in the wind, and then everyone except Deb took off their shirts and ran around like madmen. It was warm outside. The sun was out. And you could feel how warm it was. And everyone was outside in the wind. And then we went hiking.

We all found sticks. Sam's was the smallest and most maneuverable. Good for blocking and quick strike. William's was thicker and more powerful. Deb's was whippy. Mine had a sharp spike sticking out of it, which, we all agreed, would be very painful. And Lucy had this misshapen, rotten little branch that wasn't good for much of anything. "What's that do?" I asked her. "What's what do?" she said. "Your weapon," I said. "What does it do?" Lucy inspected her crooked stick. "Nothing," she said. "Look," I said, leaning in close and handing her two tiny twigs. "I have this gift for you. Use these very carefully. There is no more deadly a weapon." "What . . . what are they?" she whispered. "They are the Chopsticks of Death," I said. "You can defeat any man with these! You can even remove a man's heart while it still beats!" Lucy handled them with reverence. Michael picked up a lot of different sticks. Small twigs mostly. Good for whipping the ground with. Sam and Lucy climbed a tree. It was a pine tree, which meant it had even, straight branches. Easy for climbing. It was their first pine. "This tree's perfect for climbing," said Sam. I nodded my head sagely and told him about the big pine we had next to my house when I was a kid. And how we would always climb it. And how we always got our hands covered with pine tar. Deb, William, Michael, and I sat on the ground in the pine grove. The wind barreled through the pine boughs. "I love that sound," I said. "It sounds like a train." "Or the trees are talking to each other," said William.

Joe Blair

We hit the trail again and Sam assigned us names. I was Ogre. Sam was Leader. William was Old Man. Lucy was Woo Man. Michael, who had recently discovered the skill of clicking his tongue against the roof of his mouth, was the Clicker. Deb was the Pixie and the dog was Anonymous Boot. We were walking through the woods. We had been hiking in the lowlands and marshes near the Coralville Reservoir for more than two hours. Following streams. Sitting around in the woods. We had discovered ancient torture devices. The wind had howled. We had run. We had become covered in mud. Now we were trying to find the trailhead.

Six weary travelers.

We began our captain's log, each taking turns:

> **SAM:** The food is gone. Everyone is hungry. The Ogre has been giving me sidelong glances all day. I don't trust him.

> **WILLIAM:** The Pixie is dead. No one knows how she died. There is blood all over the Ogre's hands. I don't trust him.

> **ME:** We must carry the Pixie. Flies are gathering. The Leader has a lean and hungry look. I don't trust him.

> **SAM:** The Ogre just stabbed me in the eye. I don't trust him.

We were in stitches. Lost in the woods. But in stitches.

> **LUCY:** The Ogre is blood all over and the Old Man is died. We don't trust him.

Lucy, the five-year-old Woo Man, was trying, but William said she's not funny. She's just repeating. Lucy was undaunted.

> **Lucy:** The Old Man is stinky. We don't trust him.

Sam, Deb, and I laughed.

Once in a while, you get a day like that. A gem. You're not billing. You're not repairing furnaces. You're lost in the woods with your wife and four children and dog. The wind is strong and warm. And there's nothing else. Eventually you will find the car. And you will drive to Liberty Cones for a double scoop.

Yes, that was a good day. But it isn't today. That day happened five years ago. Sam was eleven then. Now he's sixteen. William is fourteen now. The twins are ten. We have all, since then, lost the belief in our superpowers. And Maggie, the dog, is gone. We told the kids we gave her to an old farmer and that she was on the farm now. I imagine Maggie running in a field.

The light changes and we move forward. To the left.

THE DISPLAY NEXT TO the registers reads "Viagra Substitute."

"Do you have anything like this for women?" I ask the cashier, nodding at the display.

"Those *are* for women," she says.

I place the vibrating dildo, which is packed in a plastic container with the words "Diving Dolphin" written in a wavy, blue script, on the counter along with my American Express card. It's been about one week since Deb and I argued at the Wig and Pen. That's one week without sex.

"They are?" I say. I pick up a package of the Viagra substitute, which appears to contain two pills. I scan the label. "No," I say, placing the packet of pills back in their box. "They're for men."

The cashier removes the Diving Dolphin from its package. It's a complicated looking thing with two vibrating eggs, each fitting into a separate rubber compartment. She inserts two double A's and pushes a button on the little plastic control panel. The Diving Dolphin hums loudly. "I might argue," she says.

I laugh. "Yeah," I say, "but what I need is something that makes a woman ... you know ... *want* to ... you know ... in the first place."

"We don't carry anything like that," she says. "But I know where you can get something."

"Where's that?" I say.

She motions toward the door. "Coralville Liquor Store," she says.

"They got something there?" I say.

"Yeah," she says. "Liquor."

Most guys don't want to talk about vibrating dildos. We're ashamed. But I don't know what there is to be ashamed about. If a guy could cut an hour off his commute time, he'd spare no expense to do it. And he wouldn't be ashamed to tell everyone *how* he did it. Yet everyone keeps quiet about vibrating dildos. The vibrating dildo is the time-saving device of the century.

There will come a time in your relationship when you look your wife in the eye and say, "Okay. You know I want sex. And I know you want sex. Right? Okay. So . . . what do you say we take our clothes off and both . . . just . . . get the job done. All right? And then we'll get some sleep. Okay? Because I've got to be in Cedar Rapids at seven o'clock tomorrow." Of course this approach will fail. Your wife will refuse you. No woman wants to hear these things. But just because she doesn't want to *hear* these things doesn't mean she isn't amenable to the spirit in which they're spoken.

A vibrating dildo can do lots of things that your dick can't do. It can, for example, remain in the same rigid shape for years upon years. A vibrating dildo can also vibrate. Not a bad trick, I'd say.

I told a friend of mine one time that he really should introduce the idea of the vibrating dildo to his girlfriend. He, of course, didn't want to talk about it. But I pressed the issue. "You should," I said. "Yeah." My buddy said, "I'm sure she'd be just thrilled if I pull out some giant fucking plastic thing in the middle of sex."

"Tell you what," I said. "I'll bet you a hundred bucks right now. I'm serious. A hundred bucks. That if you do pull out that giant plastic thing at the *right time*, she won't complain at all."

"Okay," he said, "Let's look at it another way: Say she likes it. Then, when I go at it the old-fashioned way again, it won't be enough. We'll have to kick-start the fucking dildo every time. What about that?"

To me, this argument holds no merit. What we're talking about here is a vibrator. It has no soul. It runs on double A's. It's not your rival. It's your helpmate. Think about the guy who rows out to sea every day. And then, after ten or twelve hours of fishing, he rows back in to shore again. One day, someone hooks him up with an outboard motor. If the guy wants to row, he can row for Christ sake. If, on the other hand, the guy has grown older and he is getting tired of rowing for fifty or sixty minutes from shore to fishing ground and back again, he can go ahead and crank up the Evinrude. His choice.

All the pressure is off. If you're afraid you won't be able to make it to shore, you have your helpmate. If your paddle seems inadequate, you have your helpmate. Your helpmate will never leave you. Your helpmate will never cheat on you. Your helpmate is there for you whenever you need it. All you need to do is remember the double A's. That's all.

When I went shopping for my first helpmate, I ended up buying a model that was an exact duplicate of an actual penis. Only larger. And purple. It was embarrassing to look at and to buy. When I brought it to the counter, I couldn't look the cashier in the eye. As if she had never sold a dildo before. As if her shop didn't have five hundred different types of dildos to choose from. Ones with big bumps all along the shaft. Little eggs with remote switches. Gigantic ones with hand cranks.

When I got home with my prize and pulled it out of the bag (right before dinner), Deb seemed put off. She didn't want to look at it. She didn't want to think about my fantastic, purple vibrating dildo. She wanted to feed the baby and give him a bath and get him to bed. In hindsight, I know I should have waited. But at the time, it seemed like it was too important to put off. I wanted her to see my dildo. *Our* dildo.

Now that I'm older, I'm much cooler about it. I don't need to buy the enormous dildo anymore. I know that a medium-size dildo will do just fine. I even ask the woman at the counter if she can plug batteries in so I can try it out. I'm like a wine connoisseur checking out an expensive bottle of Bordeaux. "Ah. A fine, tingling vibration on this one. But somewhat lacking on the lower register. Very nice. They've done a really nice job with this model. They're improving. Improving. But . . . I think I'll pass. This time. Can you bring me another dildo? Something with more . . . I don't know. Range? Yes. Exactly. Thanks. You're a doll."

I hide the Diving Dolphin in my gym bag. I figure I'll smuggle it inside and wait for the right moment to produce it.

Next, I pick up a DVD at Mr. Movie, where I end up dropping close to twenty bucks on late fees. This leaves me broke. No cash left for the liquor store. I know there will be no "special night" without alcohol. I wonder if Coralville Liquor takes American Express. I don't think they do. Then it occurs to me that I've been driving around with an old bottle of wine in my truck. A customer gave it to me a few weeks ago in exchange for a boiler inspection. I reach back to check on it and find that it's still jammed behind the passenger seat. I study the bottle. I think of the woman who gave it to me. Her name is Pamela Bell. She is a writer. She has green eyes.

"Oh!" says Deb as I'm stomping my feet on the mat after I've handed her the bottle. "You got some fancy wine! Hey. It's sort of . . . scuffed up."

"It's red," I say, tossing my gym bag down next to the back door. "Where are the kids?"

"Michelle has Mike till seven," she says. (Michelle is our respite worker. We get her for five or ten hours a week.) "Lucy's upstairs. I don't know where William is. And Sam . . . Where'd you get this?" She holds up the bottle to the light.

"The place," I say.

Deb studies the label. "The place?" she says. "What place? It looks like it's been through the mill."

"Really?" I say. "Here. Let me see."

"Where'd you get it?" says Deb, eyeing me.

"Oh," I say. "It was in my truck. A customer gave it to me."

"Customer?"

I nod, studying the label, as if looking for the answer to her question there.

"What customer?"

"Oh," I say, "some woman. I did a boiler inspection."

"What's her name?"

"I don't know."

"You don't know her name?"

"Let's see . . . ," I say. "She lives down on Lakeview. What's her name?"

Deb's arms, which have, until this moment, been resting on her hips, slip off and hang at her sides. She shakes her head. "Come on," she says.

I'm frowning and shaking my head too. Like we've both been duped somehow. "What's wrong?" I say.

"Cut the shit," she says. "Who is she?"

"I don't know," I say in an insulted voice.

"Why does this not surprise me?"

"It might . . . yeah. I think I . . . It's Pamela. Yeah. Pamela Bell. That's her name. I fixed her boiler. Or something."

"Pamela Bell," Deb says, weighing the name. "The writer?"

"Yeah. I think so."

"Oh," she says. "A writer. Is she the one you called ten times?"

"What?"

"The one you called."

"No. I told you—"

"You 'fixed her boiler'? 'Or something'? And you act like you can't—"

"Yeah," I say. "I did an inspection on—"

"Why did you act like you couldn't remember her name?"

"I wasn't acting. I couldn't—"

"So you . . . just weren't going to tell me?"

"No," I say. "It's happened before."

"I know it's happened before. That's why I'm—"

"No. I mean customers give me stuff once in a while. Remember John from John's Crane gave us all that garlic that time?"

"You remember his name pretty well."

"Yeah," I say. "John."

"Okay," says Deb. "Tell me again. What did you do for her exactly?"

"Inspected her boiler."

"And she didn't pay you because . . ."

"She wanted to," I say. "But I got the feeling she didn't have much money."

"Funny," she says. "You're suddenly a philanthropist."

"That's not fair."

"If her name was Charlie," she said. "Or Chuck. Or John. If it was John's boiler you inspected, you'd remember—"

"That's—"

"What does she look like?"

"I don't know."

"You don't know what she looks like?"

"About your height," I say. "Red hair. That's it."

"Is she pretty?"

"I don't know."

"This is just disgusting." Deb speaks each word very distinctly, as though she were dictating it to me and I was trying to take it down longhand. "This—is—just—disgusting." She's still shaking her head. She won't stop shaking her head.

"How 'bout the wine?" I say, pulling off the lead foil capsule and opening the silverware drawer. I'm looking frantically for the corkscrew. "Want some red wine? Hey, I got a good movie . . ."

"I knew it," she says. "I *knew* it."

"It's a Bruce Willis movie," I say, meaningfully.

"When did she give it to you?" she says. "When did you do the—"

"A while ago," I say. I don't look up. I'm still looking for the corkscrew. "She couldn't afford the . . . I don't know." I'm rummaging through the kitchen drawers. "Hey, did we leave that opener thing over at the Bradys' the other night?"

"Why didn't she just pay you? That is . . ."

"Like I said, she doesn't have much money. I don't know."

"Redheaded Pamela doesn't have much money."

I know my chances of getting laid are very slim now. "I don't know," I shout. "She wrote me a check but I sort of . . . Look, I don't care about all this. I don't care!" I switch tacks. It's a desperation move. "I'm innocent!" I shout. "I didn't . . ."

"Why didn't you just tell me? Why did you hide it in the—"

"I know what you think! You think there must be a *reason* why she gave me the bottle of wine! I must have 'led her on' in some way!"

"I don't think you're sleeping with her," says Deb. "But I know what you're like. You get the little titillation thing going. You gather these women. You have this little *gathering*."

"I know you're trying to . . . ," I begin. "Of course I'm not sleeping with . . . I don't care! Hey. Look. I'm innocent. I'm not going to beg for you to believe anything! If you want to be pissed off . . ."

"When do you think was the last time I put myself in the position to choose whether or not I might sleep with another guy?"

"I didn't—"

"No," she says. "No. I'm tired of this bullshit. You always need your little . . . titillation. You need your little . . . other thing."

"No. I—"

"No!" she says. "You are not faithful to me. I'm a good wife. I am. I'm a good wife and I've been putting up with this shit for a lot of years. I have always been faithful to you. Do you think I've ever—"

"A lot of years, huh?"

"That's right. I've been putting up—"

"You've been *putting up* with me, huh?"

"A lot of years and—"

"You know what our relationship is?" I say. "You know what it is? It's a series of events. You get pissed off at me and then I apologize and then—"

"Bullshit."

"And then you don't forgive me and then—"

Joe Blair

"That is such bullshit," she says. "It's more like you threaten to leave all the time and you accept bottles of wine from some slut—"

"That's such an insightful—"

"Don't try to twist it around so something's wrong with me. There's nothing wrong with—"

"It's not about right and wrong. Everything's right and—"

"There's something wrong with *you*," she shouts. "It's *you*. You know what? I have an idea. Why don't you be a man? Why don't you think about your family? Why don't you stand up and—"

"Be a man?" I say. "By that you mean 'stand up and kiss your ass twenty-four hours a day'? That's what it is. And if I were the way you want me to be, I'd never talk to anyone. And I'd be this—"

"You bring me this bottle of . . . ," she says. "Which, by the way, any woman would be hurt by. *Any woman* would be hurt. And now you're trying to—"

"I'm not trying to do anything. Listen. You're my wife. You're the one I love. Not anyone else. I don't want anyone else. I didn't want to fuck that woman. I didn't even consider it."

"It's just I'm an uptight bitch," she says, "who—"

"I'm not saying that."

"I've got some problem because I don't like it when you hang out with another woman and she gives you wine and—"

"Hey," I say. "I'm not saying you're wrong. Maybe I shouldn't have brought it in."

"*Brought it in?* How about maybe you shouldn't have—"

"We're different," I say. "You and I. We're different."

"Yeah," she says. "You can't be faithful."

"No," I say. "You hate people. You don't really talk to anyone. Everything is 'what color should I paint this wall?' and 'what do you think of my hair?' and—"

"See? You want to make me out to be some hateful, vapid person and you're—"

"I'm what? I'm what?"

"It's true. You want to make me out to be some stupid cunt and you're some freethinking—"

"Can you say that thing again?" I say. "About you being a . . . Because I didn't get it the first ten times you—"

"Fuck you," she says.

"That's good," I say. "That's—"

"Fuck you," she says.

"You know what would be cool?" I say, warming up to the idea of destroying everything. "You know what I would really love? If you went out to a bar, tonight maybe. You should! You should go out to a bar and go home with some guy and just fuck the shit out of him. No. Two guys. I mean it. Go home with two guys. That would be—"

"Why would you say that?"

"Because I want you to! Because maybe if you fucked five or ten guys, you'd climb down off your high fucking—"

"You know why I wouldn't do that? You know why? Because it goes against every grain of my being to cheat on—"

"Shit," I say.

Joe Blair

"You're a prick," she says. "You are. You're a prick. You've got a good wife, and I've been putting up with this shit—"

"Oh," I say. "There's that again. Could you just—"

"Fuck you," she says once again.

"Oh. Okay," I say. "There's that again, too. That's awesome."

"Fuck you," she says.

"Awesome."

Part Two

IT'S HARD TO ADMIT, but Pamela Bell and I have similar facial features, especially in the chin and mouth area. It's hard to admit because I'd never want to think that I'd be stricken with a reflection of myself. She called me because she wanted me to inspect her boiler. "Someone told me my boiler wouldn't last another winter," she said over the phone, "and I thought I should at least get a professional opinion."

She met me at the door and led me through the house, apologizing for the mess. And it *was* a mess. Not just in the normal scattered-dishes-and-clothing way, but in a deeply dirty and habitually disorganized way. A yellowed coffee cup with a cracked and dried substance inside was stuck to the floor beside the boiler, an eighty-year-old atmospheric thing with only two moving parts (the gas valve and the aquastat). I fired the boiler and inspected the flame, which looked exactly like a flame. I checked the flue, giving it a few pokes with my screwdriver to make sure it was solid, and then I killed the power and blew out the standing pilot in order to test the gas valve. Then I relit the pilot and ran the boiler until the water became hot enough to test the control, a beautiful antique Honeywell aquastat clamped to the supply water line. "Wow," I said. "It's still working! That's sort of amazing. You should write a letter to Honeywell or something. Maybe they'll pay you for a testimonial or something."

"Really?" she said, sincerely.

"Yeah," I said, trying to modulate my voice to something that might match her sincerity.

"Who, exactly, would I write to?"

"I don't know," I said. "I'm sure if you Googled Honeywell, they have some sort of contact for customer relations or advertising or something."

She nodded, thinking.

"Are you serious about this?" she said, after a pause. "Because I could really use the money right now, if you're serious. Or were you just trying to make conversation?"

I blinked. "Sort of trying to make conversation," I admitted.

"Because I don't want someone to just say things," she continued, as if I hadn't spoken. "Too many people say things they don't mean. It would be refreshing to meet someone who said exactly what it was they meant. I think it sucks when people sugarcoat things or try to mislead other people or say things that aren't true."

I blinked again. Something was going on. Apparently, I had disappointed Pamela Bell by being less than 100 percent sincere, and I felt compelled to make up for it. "If I were Honeywell," I said, very sincerely, "I'd be interested to know that an eighty-year-old control I manufactured was still in operation. Wouldn't you?"

She frowned and cocked her head to one side.

I twisted the handle on the old brass makeup valve and heard the rush of water through galvanized pipe. I brought up the pressure in the system to around ten pounds and then twisted the valve shut again.

"What are you doing?" she said.

"Adding water," I said.

"Why?" she said, tilting her head up to look into my eyes.

"It was just a little low," I said. I couldn't pry my eyes from her lips, which seemed to strain just a bit to cover her teeth.

"How do you know?" she said.

"The pressure," I said, pointing at the antique gauge.

"What was it?" she said.

"Around four pounds." It was a beautiful mouth.

"What should it be?" she said.

"About ten."

"Why?"

I sighed. I stopped looking at her mouth and began concentrating on her eyes, which reminded me of kiwi slices. Pamela Bell was wearing a woolen V-neck sweater that accentuated her cleavage, which was profound. And I tried very hard to be unfazed by Pamela Bell and her cleavage. Not because I'm such a culturally advanced person. Rather because I'm an old man and I wanted to convince myself that the idea of conquest had lost its luster. And even if some miracle were to have occurred and Pamela Bell were suddenly to have shown a strong interest in me, I wanted to believe that I wouldn't respond in kind. I know what goes along with sex, all of the pressing and kissing and pledges of love, and it all seems far too personal to share with someone I don't know very well. And, of course, there's the tension. Those lurking questions: How will I do? Will I win or will I lose? I want to be done with all of that nonsense. I'm a married guy and I have four children and any fleeting thrill or feeling of elation I might get out of falling in love with Pamela Bell or anyone else would be vastly outweighed by the negative circumstances that would most definitely follow. Long ago, I learned that it's easier to concentrate on sports. Or math.

Joe Blair

"You've got to figure one pound per square inch for every two point three vertical feet. So," I said, continuing before she could ask me another question, "you figure this house might be . . . what? Twenty feet high? From the boiler to the top of the highest radiator? Okay. So that's twenty divided by two point three, so you'll get something like . . ."

"Eight point six nine," she said, her throat modulating and her mouth working to cover her teeth when she spoke.

I paused for a moment. "Is that really what it is?" I said.

She didn't say anything or nod or respond in any way. She just waited for me to continue.

"Okay," I said, slightly flustered, "so, you've got about nine or so. So I just add a few pounds more than that for the hell of it, just to make sure we have a positive pressure at the highest point rather than a vacuum and . . . that's it."

Pamela nodded and almost smiled.

She followed me through the house, room to room, as I bled air from each radiator.

"What are you doing?" she said.

"Bleeding air," I said. "If there's air in the radiator, it doesn't work."

"And what's that?" she said.

"A radiator key."

"I don't have one of those."

"I'll give you this one when we're done. They're cheap. Like . . . forty cents or something. But they're kind of hard to find."

"Thank you," she said.

After we finished bleeding the radiators, we returned to the boiler and added more water.

Pamela Bell's boiler was fine. Almost perfect. The only thing wrong with it was age. And efficiency.

"Is it going to die?" she said, patting the boiler like a horse.

"Someday," I said. "But it's got some years left I think."

"You think?"

"Yes," I said. "I think."

She cocked her head and eyed me again.

"But if you want me to price you up a replacement, I'll do that."

"That's what I'd like you to do," she said. "Please."

Up the stairs.

Out to the truck.

Back into the house again, work order in hand. An old black and white dog lay unmoving in the corner of the living room. Beck was on. Dirty socks and underwear hung from the banister. Pamela wrote me a check as we stood in her cluttered foyer. She paused before handing it to me. She seemed to be waiting for something. I wanted to say, "I was in love once. But I'm not anymore. Were you ever in love?"

"No," I said. "Forget it. I didn't even do anything."

"You've got to take it," she said. "Here."

"No," I said. "It's all right."

"Don't be stupid," she said.

"Just keep it," I said. "I didn't even do anything."

Reluctantly, she withdrew the check and, in the same motion, turned and headed toward the kitchen. "Well then," she said, out of sight now, "if you're not going to take that, then at least you can take this." I heard a cabinet door open and close, and in a few seconds, she was offering me a bottle of red wine.

"Oh," I said, taking the bottle. "Thanks."

I was reaching for the doorknob when she said, "So, are you writing?"

We had spoken about college while I was bleeding the radiators. We had both been writing majors.

"Yeah," I said. "You?"

"Are you working on anything in particular?" she said.

"A book," I said. "About love. Well, not really about love. It's about this guy who has lost hope, and then finds it. And it's autobiographical, only not. And it's about faith. And a marriage that has . . . well . . . to be honest, I don't know what it's about. It's hard to say. Are you writing?"

She appeared to be amused. It almost seemed she would smile. "I'm a *writer*," she said, to clarify. "So, yes. I'm writing."

I KNEW I SHOULD HAVE thrown the bottle away. Or drunk it all by myself alone in my truck one night. Actually, I shouldn't have accepted it in the first place. I should have charged Pamela Bell the going rate for a boiler inspection. But I didn't. I didn't charge her.

After the argument, Deb storms upstairs to our bedroom, leaving me sitting in the kitchen looking out at the hard-packed patch of dirt in our backyard. People ask about it all the time, the patch of dirt where grass won't grow. They also wonder about the hasp and padlock on the refrigerator. They wonder why the gate on our six-foot-high picket fence is permanently bolted shut. Deb and I hardly think about these things. We've been with Michael for ten years now.

There are two runways inside the fence. One traces the edge of the house. The dog made this one. He sprints from window to window, tracking my location. Am I in the kitchen? Am I leaving the kitchen? Am I walking to the living room? Am I walking back to the kitchen? D'Artagnan's head pops up in each window as I pass. I might consider this cute if it weren't for the destroyed windowsills and muddy paw prints on the siding.

The other runway belongs to Michael. It's a ten-by-three stretch of shiny earth in the center of our tiny backyard. There are three layers of sod beneath it, each one representing Deb's hope that this time the grass will take hold. This time the grass will take hold. This time . . .

Once she placed wrought-iron deck chairs over the spot, but Mike moved them. One time a heavy picnic table. But it blocked all the sunlight and the grass almost died anyway. So we moved the table and Mike finished the job with his pacing.

First thing in the morning, whether at 2:00 A.M. or 6:00 A.M. or 8:00 A.M., you can depend on Mike to find one of my leather belts, sneak out the back door, and start walking back and forth over his little patch of dirt, hard and solid on dry days, loose and slick on rainy days. What could be better? A belt that, if you bend at the waist and move your arm back and forth at a certain pace, will make sine wave after sine wave, the tail of the belt lapping the ground ever so gently as it releases the previous wave into the universe. It is a mesmerizing thing. So absorbing. So incredibly fantastical that Mike can't help but release shrieks of delight. Or agony. Or pent-up frustration. Or joy. In that muddy patch. In that sinusoidal belt. In that release into the universe. He is the near-supersonic Tarzan. The alarm clock that cannot be ignored. At least Deb and I can't ignore him, because we do have neighbors—one old veterinarian and his wife, one guy who is the head of some department or other at the University of Iowa and his wife, who is a teacher at West High, and another guy who works in the penal system. Michael will be naked. Or he will have boxer shorts on. He will be screaming or singing or howling in a shatteringly high pitch. Like a seagull only much higher and much louder and more prolonged. And one of us, Deb or me, cursing beneath our breath, will peel ourselves out of bed and hurry down the creaking stairway. "Michael!" we will say in our most authoritative voice. "Michael. Get in here!" And Michael will drop his belt and do as we say. He will leave behind the thing he loves the most. More than food. And he will do what we say. Until we are back in bed. And then he will return to his beautiful runway. With his magical belt. And he will make the world understandable. In a sinusoidal way.

When Mike first saw the open water, two summers ago on East Beach in San Francisco, he was enthralled. He threw himself on the sand, which was warm and fine, and listened to the sound of the surf. It was as if he had finally found someone who spoke his language. The sea. Source of all sine waves. Mother of all repetition. We visited East Beach every day for five days, but this was only vacation. And despite what little boys want, vacations end. Soon, Mike was back in Iowa and it was the belt again, lapping against the brick walkway while he waited for the school bus with his mom and dad.

"The teachers will think I'm stupid," said Lucy. "Like Mike."

"Mike is not stupid!" said Deb.

"Mom," said Lucy, patiently. "You know what I mean."

"Yes," said Deb. "I know what you mean. But you've got to know what I mean, too. Imagine if you found yourself in the middle of China somewhere. And everyone was trying to talk to you. But you couldn't understand them. And everyone thought you were stupid. But you were still just like you are. How would you feel?"

Sometimes, I get angry at Mike. And then, having failed the test yet again, I feel bad about it. "Michael!" I'll shout, when I find him hunched on the toilet seat, hand shoved between his legs, an entire roll of crumpled, poop-smeared toilet paper strewn around the room. "Michael!" I'll shout. "Get your hand out of your butt! You don't stick your hand in your butt! Come here. Let's wash your hands, Mike!" and Mike will do as I say. He will stop doing the marvelous thing and he will allow his hands to be washed. And then, after his hands are clean, the way I wanted them to be, and I have returned to doing whatever it is I was doing, he will begin to dig once again. Exploring that ever-fascinating cavity.

I have had glimpses of the kind of man I should be. Such are the revelations we are afforded. Passing glimpses, like small, hidden ponds you pass by on your motorcycle while driving on a road you've never traveled before, a pine forest suddenly opening up and then closing once again, that secret pond instantly forgotten or recalled only in part. I have had these glimpses. Once, while attending some frighteningly capitalistic rally for Amma, the hugging saint, her face magnified and simulcast throughout the convention center in Coralville, and printed on mugs and glossy paper and everything else, I had a glimpse. Deb had the idea that a hug from Amma would somehow save Mike. As if a hug could heal the lesions on his brain. I did not believe in the powers of the hugging saint. I did not believe that Mike would benefit from her blessing. Or the glazed-over smiles of her myriad followers. Or the hypnotizing chants. I wanted nothing more than to get my son, who was lying on the floor, feeling the carpet with his lips and screaming, outside and in the car, where I could maybe listen to the Cubs game. And then, while I was hauling Michael to his feet, Amma's interpreter came on the dozens of flat-screen monitors and said something about eternity. And then he said something about kindness. I had my arms locked around Mike's chest, preventing him from flopping on the carpet, and I was pulling him along in the direction of the exit. People streamed past us. Beads and eye makeup. Saris and stocking feet. Michael caught the eye of more than a few convention goers. One man, who was wearing a white robe, smiled at him and gave a slight bow.

A woman with a red bindi in the center of her forehead stopped and bowed even lower. Michael received many bows on our way out to the truck. It was as if these people recognized Michael as a visiting deity from another world.

When I was ten years old, I would pray to God and ask for my challenge. "Give me my challenge," I would pray. "Give me my challenge." In my weaker moments I think that this was my mistake. I had asked for it, after all.

I rarely spend much time talking to Mike because he rarely responds in any way. You may think this is cruel, ignoring my own son. And if you were to spend one day with him, you might be full of energy and hope and goodwill. But Mike is ten years old. And I have been with him every day of his life. I repeat the bad habit I have acquired of ignoring my son so often, my time with him has become a series of responses that have been followed, step by step. They have become something of a runway. I ignore the seemingly meaningless words that he repeats. I ignore the very things that fascinate my son. The belt. The patch of dirt.

Still, once in a while, we engage one another.

Tonight, for example, we play the blinking game. While we are lying next to one another, very close, Mike looks at me out of the corner of his eye, a sly smile playing across his face, and he blinks once. Then, in response, I blink once. His smile gains in radiance. And he answers my blink with one blink of his own. This goes on for some time, whipping him up into a fit of laughter. Having found my bedroom door locked, I continue to lie next to Mike. It's eleven o'clock. Well past his bedtime. He has been nervous. Maybe he has broken into the fridge again and eaten some of the food that is forbidden him by his gluten-free, dairy-free diet. He has been laughing hysterically for at least an hour, which might seem adorable to you but to me indicates that he is on the edge of a seizure. Our faces are very close in the dark. Mike likes it this way. Close. He is a beautiful boy. His eyes are large and liquid. His facial features are clean. "Mike," I say in the darkness, "you're a good kid." I say it, and then I listen, for once. I don't stop listening after a few seconds but let the seconds run on. Mike has ceased his laughter now. After some time, I don't know how long, Mike whispers very quietly, "You're" and "a good kid." And then, "A good." And then, "Kid." And then "Mike, you're a good kid."

"I'm proud of you," I whisper. The words wave and wave. And then they come back. Broken and then full. "Proud," says Michael. "I'm proud of you."

"I love you," I say. It's a profession. And it's also a self-rebuke. "Love," says Mike, after a few minutes. "I love you. Love you. I love. I love you. You."

"How would you like to move to a place by the ocean?" I say, after Mike seems to be done with his response. This brings a big smile from Mike. He is looking off. Away. At something far. The words wave and wave. "Ocean," he says.

The people who visit our house don't understand the runway. Or the locks on the refrigerator. They don't understand nor do they want to understand nor is it theirs to understand. It has not been given to them. It has been given to us. The great challenge I had asked for, imagining the crack of doom and the Argonauts and the twelve labors of Hercules, is lying in his bed and very close to my face. Faith is nothing other than an acceptance of eternity and, at the same time, of death. The great challenge, my great challenge, is nothing more than, in the face of eternity and death, a question of kindness. Can I, being alive at this time, love this boy? Can I listen to him? Can I be a good father to this boy?

For the moment, it's clear to me. I can visualize the man I should be. But soon, it's hidden by sleep. And the rushing pine trees of my dreams and the hills of Massachusetts and laundry baskets and the loud machines of my trade that demand so much. And the ocean that was once many rivers. And the rivers that were once many clouds filled with rain.

THE FOLLOWING EVENING WHEN Mike goes down for the night, we post Sam and William across the hall to watch a DVD in our bedroom and we head for the Wig and Pen. The bar is crowded with volunteers who have been building a sandbag levee to protect the floodplain neighborhood known as Mosquito Flats from the rising waters of the Iowa River.

"I'm sorry, baby," I say. "I'm sorry, but—"

"No," says Deb. "I'm sorry."

"You didn't do anything."

"I did. I'm always so—"

"But what I want to say is—"

"—jealous," she says.

"We've got to do something," I say.

"What do you want to do?"

"I don't know. Don't you think we've got to do something?"

"Come on!" someone shouts. It's a familiar voice. We both turn to look. We recognize a friend of ours named Peter Lawler. He's seated at a small table near the entrance, his back to us.

"Capone!" he shouts. "Capone! No! You've got to *say* it!"

Peter is a boyishly handsome man. A college professor. Fiftyish years old. He has a quality about him that appeals to both men and women. I don't know what quality that is, exactly. But he has it. He has, I guess you could say, a way about him that makes you sincerely believe that he thinks you are special and that the things you say are interesting and that the way you look is appealing.

The water levels are predicted to peak by the end of the week, and everyone is talking about the flood. Peter is dressed in shorts and a T-shirt although the outside temperature is in the low fifties. The bar seems especially ebullient and loud, the patrons celebrating their most recent round of sandbagging.

There's a TV above the bar. It's the third inning of the first game of a Red Sox–Yankees three-game series. The score is tied zero to zero in the second, and Peter is playing some sort of drinking game with two undergraduate-age women. "Come on, Dick!" shouts Peter, addressing the bar owner, a stoic, chain-smoking man who rarely leaves his shadowy corner table. "You'll love it. Come on! It's right out of 1985. Come on!"

"No thanks," says Dick, coolly, cigarette in hand. "I think I've heard enough people shouting *Capone* for one night."

"Come on!" shouts Peter. "Come on!"

"Nineteen eighty-five?" says one of the coeds to the other. "We weren't even *born* then!"

"What's he doing?" says Deb.

"We should leave him alone," I say.

"But, what's he doing?" she says.

"Looks like he's trying to get laid," I say.

"It *does* look like that," says Deb, shaking her head. "Why would he do that? Jessica is so beautiful."

"Just leave him be," I say. "He probably doesn't want those girls to know he's friends with old people like us."

Bobby Abreu hits a chopper to Dustin Pedroia. Pedroia scoops it up and makes the throw to first.

"I can't do it anymore," I declare over the din, getting back to the *marital strife* part of the conversation. "I think . . . I think . . ."

Loud laughter.

Clattering trays.

"We just keep repeating the same things over and over!" I say.

"Yeah," says Deb. "That's life."

"Yeah?" I say. "Well I don't like it."

"We have children, Joe," says Deb. "It's not all about you anymore. It's not—"

"*Anymore?* It's not about me *anymore?* That's funny. That's a riot."

"It's true."

"You keep saying the same thing. 'It's not about you anymore.'"

"Yeah," says Deb. "It's not. It's about the children."

"And we're doing them this big favor by—"

"We're *married*, Joe," she says. The way she says it admits no rebuttal. But, having already downed two pints of Bass, I don't much care what she might or might not admit.

"I don't care," I say. "You said you thought I didn't love you. That's not true. But, I think maybe you want it to be true. Because then you could . . ."

"So, your answer is . . . what?" says Deb. "You want to sleep with other women. That's—"

"That's not—" I begin.

"You want to sleep with other women," she says again.

"No," I say. "Absolutely not. But . . . what if I did?"

"I knew it!" she shouts, almost victoriously. "Why do you—"

"No! No! You don't understand! It's not about sex. It's not. It's about . . . love."

"You want to leave me."

"No. That's not what I'm saying. I just want us both to . . . choose again. To . . . be loved. And to love. You know? I'm trying—"

"And you think that, by threatening me you can—"

"I'm not threatening you."

"You think I stop you from—"

"You do!" I say. "You do stop me! You know . . . how many friends do I have?"

"You think I stop you from . . ."

"How many friends do I have?"

"Matt . . ."

"Please."

"Matt's your friend."

"Matt? Matt's an acquaintance."

"Ethan?"

"I see Ethan . . . what? Once every other month? He's always on the road or something."

"So, what's your point?"

"You're all I have!"

"What's so bad about that?"

"You don't even . . . *like* me!" I say. "That's pretty fucking sad. Don't you think?"

Deb shrugs, scanning the crowd.

"I need . . . more," I say. "Don't you?"

"No," she says, still scanning. "I don't."

"Well, then that's the difference between us. You're . . . way up there on the high . . . thing. Horse. List. Whatever. But I can't accept this . . . life we've got going on here. I want to love someone. Maybe a lot of people. I want to talk to them and write and . . . have dinner and an actual conversation with someone. Whatever. But you don't want to do that with me and you don't want me doing anything with anyone else because—"

"That's not fair!" she says, now eyeing me angrily. "That's not—"

"How often do I play golf?"

"*What?*"

"I love golf. You know that?"

"Not golf again! Oh, dear God! This is ridiculous! What are you, five?"

"I love golf. And I played . . . twice last year. I don't care, really. But you know how angry you get when I play golf?"

"That's not true!"

"Remember last time I played? We got in that big fight. We didn't talk for three days. And I only played—"

"I know. Twice."

"You don't want me writing with Pamela. Or Lauren. Or—"

"You're writing with Pamela?"

"No," I say. "I'm just using her for—"

"The Blairs!" shouts Peter, now standing next to our table, seemingly oblivious to our rising emotions. Peter's arms are outstretched. He is smiling his perfect, sincere-seeming, boyish smile. "What the hell are you guys doing here?" he says. "Come here! Bring it in!" He leans down and embraces me roughly.

"That's his boyfriend," I hear one of the very young women say to the other.

He then leans over and gives Deb a big hug.

"That's his girlfriend," I hear the other very young woman say. They giggle.

"How long have you guys been here?"

"I don't know," I say. We all look at the pitcher of Bass. It's nine-tenths empty. "About that long," I say.

"I didn't see you!" shouts Peter. "Didn't you see me? I was sitting right over there next to the door! I was—"

"We saw you," says Deb. "But we didn't want to blow your gig."

"My gig? My *gig*? Please!" He laughs loudly. "They're fifteen years old! Give me a break!"

Peter plops himself down between us and takes another swallow of beer. "I can't believe you've been here for half an hour and you didn't even tell me. I don't care where Joe is. I don't care if he's getting a lap dance in a strip club. I'd come right up to him and say, '*Hey, Joe! Joe Blair!*' Hey, let me buy you guys another pitcher. Hey, CQ! CQ! Hey, CQ! Could you get these guys a pitcher of . . ."

"Bass," Deb and I say simultaneously.

"Bass," says Peter. "A pitcher of Bass? Thanks, Q! Q's all right. So what are you guys doing here? Watching the game? Deb, you are so beautiful." He leans over and gropes for her hand. Finds it. Holds it. "You are. You are so beautiful. So, why didn't you guys tell me you were here?" He's still holding Deb's hand.

"You probably can't tell," says Deb, making no effort to remove her hand from Peter's, "but we're in a fight."

"A fight? What are you fighting about?"

"Freedom," I say. "I think every ten years—"

"Don't listen to him!" says Deb, reclaiming her hand. "He'll give you a biased view—"

"So," says Peter, "what? Every ten years . . . what?"

"The bonds of marriage should . . . what did I say? Expire? Can bonds expire?"

"Uh-oh," says Peter. "You want . . ."

"Love."

"Love?" he says, laughing. "What kind of love are you talking about?"

"All kinds," I say. "Golf—"

"Not golf again!" says Deb. She's getting drunk. I can tell by her volume.

"What, then?" says Peter, eyeing Deb.

"He wants to have sex with other women," she says.

I roll my eyes. "I don't."

"He does. That's why he's been trying to get me to sleep with other guys."

"Really?" says Peter, shifting his focus to me.

I shake my head.

"He has," she says. "He thinks that'll clear the way for him to . . ."

"That's not true," I say. "I think . . . what my point is . . . what I'm trying to say is, I think it's important that we don't sin against—"

"Dude," says Peter. "You can't use that word."

"What word is that?"

"*Sin*. That word cannot be used."

"What I was—"

"I'm just kidding," says Deb. "He doesn't want that. He never said that."

Peter nods, suddenly disinclined to talk.

The Red Sox, who were tied with the Yankees at one apiece in the fifth, now find themselves down by two in the eighth. The Yankees have the bases loaded, which attracts my attention until Jose Molina strikes out to end the inning. Meanwhile, Deb and Peter have been deep in conversation. At some time around midnight, when Pedroia lines out to end the game, there seems to be a universal agreement among the patrons that it's time to go. We stand with the rest of them.

"He can't drive," says Deb, jabbing her finger into Peter's chest. "Hey, you"—she jabs him again—"can't drive!"

"You're not driving," I say to Peter.

"That's probably a good idea," he says.

"Okay," I say. "We'll take you home."

"But my Mercedes," he says.

"I'll bring you to your car in the morning."

"Mercedes."

"What?"

"You said car. It's not a *car*. It's a—"

"Okay. I'll bring you here."

"That was a joke," he says, "about the Mercedes. It's supposed to be . . . a joke. Hey, are you sure?"

"About what?"

"You can bring me back here?"

"Sure," I say.

"Sure?" he says. "Sure? Okay. Bye, Dick! Bye, CQ!"

Joe Blair

They say the downtown bridges over the Iowa River will soon be closed because of the rising water. Dubuque Street is already closed. After I cross the Park Street Bridge, I stop the car and consider my options. "Should I try to go through town?" I say. "Or back through Coralville?" The beautiful water is everywhere and time seems skewed in a dramatic way. We could be living in another century. There is still power to the white lights that illuminate the path along the river where the kids and I have walked d'Artagnan so often. The lights are large and perfectly round and perfectly white like dozens of fallen moons. The kids and I used to make up stories about the lights. We said there was a war between the white ones and the yellow ones. The white ones owned all the territory around the river and all the bridges, but the yellow ones owned the city. And there was a mighty battle. And it was pretty even until the moon came down and broke the stalemate and then the white lights won.

"It's your freedom," says Deb. "You're the freedom guy. Isn't that what you want?"

"Deb," says Peter, "get back here."

"No," says Deb. "I'm fine."

"Come on," he says. "Don't be that way. Get back here. I just want to talk. Come on." He grabs her wrist gently. Deb shoots me a questioning look, but I pretend I don't see. I stare straight ahead at the road.

"Okay," says Deb and blithely steps over the divider into the backseat.

"Great," says Peter. "Great. Hey, Joe, could you turn up the music?"

I take the long way around the detour. Despite the music, I can hear rubbings and small moanings. This goes on for a minute or two. Suddenly Deb is back in the passenger seat.

"You okay?" I say quietly.

"Oh," she says, "I'm fine." And then she says, below the music, "It's dangerous back there."

"Really?" I say.

I continue to drive.

I'm surprised at how excited I am by my wife crossing over into the
backseat. I'm also surprised by my total lack of jealousy.

"Deb . . . ," I say quietly.

"Joe . . . ," says Deb loudly and brightly, defying my attempted secrecy. "So,"
she says, addressing Peter, "how's your job? I hear you're . . . in charge of a
whole new . . . what? Department or something? That's so exciting!"

There is a stretch of silence from the backseat.

"Deb?" says Peter. "Could we not . . . talk for a while? If I've done
something . . . idiotic? Could you just let me . . ."

"Peter," says Deb, "you know we love you. You couldn't do . . ."

Suddenly, Peter is sitting between us on the console. He's leaning toward
my wife. He's saying things to her. Very low in her ear. I can hear her let
out a little moan. He's kissing her again. I can barely keep the car on the
road. I'm overtaken by a desire to see my wife transform into someone
other than the woman I thought I knew her to be. Someone else. With
brightly colored wings, maybe. Someone who might surprise me. "Come
on," says Peter, pulling at Deb's hand. "Come on. It's fine." He withdraws
from the console and settles back into his seat. He's leading my wife. She
follows. She steps over the console again, still holding Peter's hand. "Deb,"
I say. She glances at me and then away. "Deb," I say again, "you don't have
to—" Deb glares at me as she settles into the backseat.

Joe Blair

All around is darkness. The dam at the reservoir is very close to overflowing. There has been an uprising. The water is rioting. I drive. A New York group called Spottiswoode and His Enemies is on. They're singing a sad song about a troubadour. The troubadour was once young. All the women wanted him. But now he plays birthday parties because he's cheaper than a clown. I discover new routes through North Liberty I have never known to exist.

Another man put his hands on my breasts," breathes Deb. The bedroom is absolutely black. Rain beats against the glass like it wants to get in. I'm still shaking with adrenaline. The whole thing still seems impossible. It's as if we crossed the line between life and death and then back again. And it was easy. There was no crashing of cymbals or flashes of lightning. There was no voice of God.

"Really?" I say.

"Yes," she says.

We move together.

"It's what you wanted," she says. "Right?"

"I don't know."

"Did you want it?"

"Yes. I guess so."

We continue.

"Love shouldn't be wasted," she says. "Should it?"

"No," I say.

Pause.

Joe Blair

"It's only our bodies," she says. "Right?"

"I think so," I say. "I think you're right."

"Yes," she says. "It's only our bodies."

We move together.

"Well?" I say. "Did you . . . like it?"

"Yes," she whispers. "I did."

"You liked it?"

"Uh-huh," she says.

"What did you do?"

She twists her body beneath me. We pause.

"He told me I was beautiful. I know it's not true . . ."

"But it is true, Deb. It is true. You are so beautiful."

"I know it's not true," she says again. "That's just what he says so women will want to . . ."

"What'd you do?"

"You didn't look back?"

We are moving again. "No," I say.

"He told me he'd always wanted to sleep with me. He said he always has. I know it's bullshit. And when I told him I'd never even kissed another man since I've been married, I think he started to cry."

"He cried?"

"Yeah," she says. "I think so."

"So," I say, "what did you do?"

"Nothing," she says.

"You did *something*."

Deb is silent, moving violently against me now.

"It's okay," I say.

I'm so turned on, it's hard to keep from coming.

"It's okay," I say again.

"What do you want me to say?" she breathes.

"The truth," I say.

"We just . . . ," she whispers, "kissed. That's all." The words are barely audible.

I need to stop again. Our bodies are slippery with sweat. But Deb won't let me stop. She moves beneath me with incredible need. She won't stop. Something has shaken loose in her. I think this is the moment. I reach under my pillow.

"What's that thing?"

"It's a Diving Dolphin," I say.

"Oh," she says. "How does it . . . work?"

"I'm not sure," I say, fumbling with the remote. "I think there are . . . different settings or something."

I'M AT THE STARBUCKS on Clinton Street in Iowa City waiting for Pamela. Deb does not know I'm here and I don't plan on letting her know. It's two days since the incident with Peter in the backseat of the minivan and the second time Pamela and I have met since I inspected her boiler. The first time, Pamela interviewed me for an article she was writing on the parents of special needs children. This time, I told her I wanted to teach her to do what my friend Mary Allen calls a fast-write, where you sit down and write like crazy for an hour or so, not giving a shit if it's any "good" or not, and then reading what you've just written aloud to one another. We agreed to meet at one o'clock, but I showed up early, thinking I might cheat and get something half decent down before she arrived, but there's nothing to write, really. I mean, what the fuck am I doing? I could be doing something worthwhile. It's not like I *want* to write. In fact, I avoid it like the plague. Of course, you can't really avoid the plague. You can try, but you can't avoid it.

I base this in-depth knowledge of the plague on a short story by Edgar Allan Poe, where a bunch of courtiers drop dead of the "Red Death" after barricading themselves in a palace ballroom. They all got some kind of plague, which sounds a lot like Ebola with all the blood leaking out all over the place. Either you get a plague or you do not. I got it.

Joe Blair

I look around the Starbucks and there's a woman standing just inside the entrance. She's wearing very high heels and loose-fitting pants. She is slender and stylish. Her ensemble is white and blue. She is of the age where you'd say she is "well preserved." By this I mean she looks to have had some help in the breast department and face department. But who am I to say? She is near fifty. She seems to be waiting for someone and she seems perturbed.

A good-looking man wearing shorts that are cut above his knees (not very stylish according to my sons) and leather sandals and a button-up cotton shirt bursts through the door and pulls the well-preserved woman into a passionate embrace. He has a full head of hair and straight teeth and a tan. He is now embracing the woman who was waiting but is no longer waiting. I try not to look at them, but I can't help it. He is kissing her face. Her lips. Her eyes. Her cheeks. The embrace goes on too long for her liking, but he doesn't notice. Either that, or he doesn't care. She has released him, but he continues to embrace her, this good-looking, well-coiffed man who is somewhere in his middle age. He holds on to her as though she were his youth. These two are obviously not married. This kind of desperation doesn't happen with married couples unless they are fresh on the heels of a separation or have recently cheated. The man and woman sit across a small table from one another holding hands, both hands, and leaning forward. Every few seconds, the handsome man leans across the table and kisses the well-preserved woman passionately. He doesn't care who might see. She never leans forward to kiss him. He's the one doing all the work. I'm thinking, Cool it, man. You're going to blow it! I'm thinking this guy should know this by now. You can't be too enthusiastic. Especially when she's not. It's bound to fail. No matter how handsome you might be.

I'm thinking I should write something about how great it is that this guy is so passionate. What a beautiful thing it is. But I can't help but feel a little bit sickened by him. I'm not trying to eavesdrop, but they're sitting at the next table over and I can hear him mention something about his wife. And something about divorce. I don't want to think about it, but I think about these two banging. Just banging away for hours probably, with the help of incredible new drugs. I don't want to think about these things and I certainly don't want to write about them, but I'm dying of the plague and I can't help it.

The word *passion* is from the Latin *passionem*, which means "suffering, enduring." What else could the word *passion* mean? "Good times"? "Happiness"? Passion has nothing to do with happiness. Even though this guy seems happy, I don't think he is. I think he's . . . something else. But what do I know? Maybe this guy is the happiest son of a bitch on the planet and I don't want to believe it because I'm such a negative person.

I think it's safe to assume this, though: that the handsome man really wants to be happy. I think we all want to be happy. I also think we rarely are. Happiness, like the urge to write, is a virus we catch. Not on purpose, but randomly. It comes, displays its symptoms, and then it goes. And we're left with a type of wistful nostalgia for this fleeting, accidental thing. This is our most common stance in the world. It's not a balanced pose, rather a kind of suffering. Enduring. A kind of passion. Which, we all agree, is a positive thing. For some reason. We want to be passionate. And we want to be happy. It's sort of like wanting to be sick and well at the same time.

This is what I'm thinking about when Pamela walks in. She is wearing a green cotton button-up shirt and blue pants. She sets up her computer across from me in a businesslike way, with very little small talk involved. Only the very basics. "Hello. How are you? I'm getting a coffee. You want anything?"

It doesn't take long before she has her coffee and is, once again, sitting across from me. "Before we start," she says, leaning in, "I just want to ask: when you were over at the house? You said something about *peace work*. You said being a parent is *peace work?*" She is wearing starfish earrings.

"Yeah," I say.

"Did you mean piecework—p-i-e-c-e? Or the other way: p-e-a-c-e?"

"P-i-e-c-e," I say. "Like a . . . millwright or something."

"Oh," she says, disappointed. "I liked it when it was the other. I guess I don't understand what you mean." She is wearing dull red lipstick.

I try to look like I'm concentrating. "It's like," I say, "you only get paid for what you do. Like, five cents a . . . cobblestone. Or whatever."

"I know what *piecework* means," she says. "But I don't know how it relates to *parenthood*."

"Oh," I say, frowning. "Well, maybe I meant it the other way."

After five or ten minutes of this, I explain the exercise and we open our laptops and begin to write. We continue on for about an hour. When I finish with a flourish of especially hard keystrokes and then look up from my screen, Pamela is still going like mad. She holds up her index finger between words. "One minute," she says, almost angrily.

I wait, spending my time closing my document and saving it and then staring at my screen saver. Homer Simpson is mowing a lawn. Dandelions keep popping up.

I glance at Pamela. She's still going like crazy.

These things never end well. Do they? You can't do things like this. Can you? I think of New England. I think of the poet Donald Hall, who moved back to the farmhouse in New Hampshire where he was raised. I wonder if he felt that he had pulled off an impossible trick. Cancer aside. The death of his wife aside. Donald Hall and Jane Kenyon had about twenty years there in that old farmhouse together. I wonder if it was the place they needed it to be. Home.

When Pamela finally quits typing, I pull out my phone and place it on the table. "This is how we usually do it," I explain, and spin the phone. The antenna points in Pamela's direction. "Okay," I say. "You first."

She reads what she has written. It's about a wedding in Bangladesh. "The world," she writes, "is larger than we can know. It's an immense, gesticulating place. Hindus spread their prayer mats and pray. One hundred and fifty flower girls reach into their baskets and toss rose petals on the Astroturf. Tiger sharks approach the shore, turn, and swim uncertainly back out to sea." She finishes with a tiny image. Of her tiny self, lying in bed beside her tiny dog. The surf repeats a single word to them. The surf never stops repeating the word. It's the word that will explain everything to us. And we try, but we can't understand what it means.

"Um . . . ," I say. "That was . . . un-fucking-believable." Her eyes remain locked on mine. They do not change in size or shape. "I mean it," I say. "That was . . . world-class. Amazing. Really, really amazing. With the sharks? And the . . . the Astroturf and everything? Amazing. The whole thing just opened up, and then, suddenly, shrank back down. Very moving, really."

She nods. "Thanks," she says. "Now you."

I swallow. I've written two short pieces. I know I can't read the first thing I wrote about the good-looking guy and passion and happiness and the plague. That would be cheating. Besides, it's a little too close to home. And my second piece on repairing a chiller at Winneshiek Hospital in Decorah, Iowa, and then driving to Walmart seems less than adequate. But I'm stuck. She showed hers, now I need to show mine. "Nick is nice. Too nice. I never trusted him," I begin, cringing. The essay doesn't get any better from here. I describe Nick: "A broad-shouldered guy with the look of a mafia hit man." I describe the mechanical room at the hospital: "neat and clean and everything freshly painted machine gray." I explain that I'm repairing a chiller and I can't get a bolt loose. So I need to get an extension for my wrench. It still won't come, so I get a longer extension. I lean on it with all my strength. The bolt breaks in two. This is the big turning point in the essay. The Cubs game is on the radio. There are no sharks. No Hindus. No one is throwing rose petals. I'm driving my work van to Walmart, that well-lit bastion of organization and regularity. When I read the last sentence, "Why do the bananas frighten me so?" Pamela frowns. "I don't get it," she says.

"Don't get what?" I say.

"The whole thing," she says. "I mean, here's a guy working on a piece of equipment, and then he drives to Walmart."

"Yeah?"

"I don't get it."

"Maybe there's nothing to get," I say. "I mean . . . I just wrote the fucking thing five minutes ago. I can't really explain it to you."

She nods professionally.

THE CONCEPT OF FIDELITY confuses me. Why, for example, should two people hold one another hostage where sex is concerned? It's ridiculous. Like the Iowa law that allows gambling only if it happens on a boat. Where is the sense in it? If a wife is bored by talking to her husband, why should she need to talk to him every night? If a wife doesn't want to sleep with her husband anymore, why should she be expected to limit herself to him? How did this absurd arrangement we call fidelity begin? Why this mutual hostage taking? Why continue to do things the way we have always done them? Why not, instead, revolt? Why not reach down into the basement and find every last book, every last photo album, every last Christmas decoration and piece of sports memorabilia and crayon drawing and extra furnace filter and destroy them? Why not be part of a force that ruins everything?

"You ever get the feeling," my friend Bernie said, leaning on his driver, while waiting to tee off on the fourth hole at Finkbine Golf Course, "that everyone is fucking everyone else except you?"

"Yeah," I said. "Why?"

"I don't know," he said. "I just think it's true. You know Gill? From my office? You met him at that poker game. Yeah. Gill. You know him. Gill. He's been fucking some other dude's wife."

"Yeah?" I said.

"Yeah," said Bernie. "And not only is his wife okay with it, she's *fucking the other dude.*"

"Really?" I said.

"Yeah. And I was talking to Cindy? The bartender over at the Nickelodeon? And . . . she hears this kind of stuff all the time, by the way . . . this one couple? They're talking about taking a trip to Vegas together? And they start talking about *their spouses.* The dude says his wife might have something planned that weekend, and the chick says her husband will be home at that time. You know what I mean? It's happening all around us! It'd be one thing if it was New York City or something and no one knew anyone, but this is Iowa City, man! These are regulars, right? And everyone knows they aren't married, and they aren't even trying to *hide* it!"

"Really?" I said.

"Yeah," he said. "So, in conclusion, I'd just like to say"—he stepped between the tee box markers—"everyone's out there getting laid."

I nod, staring off, starry-eyed and forlorn. "Except us," I said.

"Except us," he said, nodding firmly and teeing up his ball, a Titleist Pro V1 with a little red mark beneath the logo to prove who the ball belongs to.

"I don't know, Deb," I say. "I just think it shouldn't matter."

The bedroom again. Darkness. Rain is pounding against the windows. We're going at it again, for the fourth time in the two days since the backseat incident.

"You don't?"

"No," I say. "I think we're entering a whole new . . . thing. What do you call it?"

"Era?"

"Era. That's it." I pause, out of breath. "I think we're entering a whole new era here. Of sex. Don't you think?"

"I don't really want to talk about it."

"I'm just kidding," I say. "This is all just . . . fantasy talk. Okay? It's not even real. I just thought it might . . . you know. Be good." I take a few more gulps of air and then begin again.

"So," I continue, "what do you want to do?"

"Um," she says, "what we're doing is fine."

"No, I mean, this being fantasy, I'm talking fantasy here, what do you want to do? Out of everyone we know, who would you . . ."

"No one," she says.

"Come on," I say. "I'm trying to play this new fantasy thing and you're talking like we're in court or something."

"Okay," she says. "I'll try."

"Okay," I say.

We continue on for a while.

"You know," I say, "Kurt and I already talked about it."

"About what?"

"You know," I say.

"You didn't talk about that with Kurt!" she says, too loudly. "Besides, you think I'd want to sleep with *Kurt?* That's kind of insulting. That's like me asking you to sleep with . . . I don't know . . . Melissa *Barth* or something."

I laugh. "No," I say. "No. I don't . . . Deb, can you at least . . ."

"Okay," she says. "Sorry."

"So," I say. "I'm just saying. He is just downstairs."

This is not part of the fantasy thing. This is true. The Coralville Dam flooded the spillway yesterday and my friend Kurt needed to move out of his place as a precaution, so I told him we could put him up in our basement. We loaded all of his belongings into a truck and hauled them all to a temporary storage place in North Liberty.

"I know that," says Deb.

"And we already talked about it, me and him."

"You didn't talk about it, Joe."

"Yes, we did."

We fall silent and soldier on for a while.

"Do you want to know what he said?" I say.

"Are we playing fantasy right now, or . . ."

"Yes. This is total fan—"

"Okay. What did he—"

"He says he's always wanted to. . . . With you."

"Really?"

"Yeah."

"Aw," she says. "That's . . . real nice."

"Yeah, and he said . . . he said . . . um . . . should I go get him?"

"No!"

"Deb . . . remember . . . this is just . . ."

"Okay," she says, after a pause. "I'm sorry. Sure."

"Sure what?" I say. "Sure, I should go get him? Or . . ."

"Yes," she says. "Sure. Go get him."

"He's just downstairs," I say.

"All right!" she says. "What else do you want me to say?"

"Okay," I say. "I'll go get him."

"I know. I know. You already said that."

This isn't working like I had hoped. Not that I had planned it out. But there seems to be something more required of me in regard to this fantasy game. Maybe more imagination. But I don't have any more imagination and I ran out of things to say almost from the start. Dr. Ruth says fantasy is healthy. That's what she says. But I have to wonder, as everyone who has ever taken advice from Dr. Ruth must wonder, whether she has any firsthand experience in these matters. Here's what I suspect is the truth about fantasy: it wants nothing more than to become reality. It's like Pinocchio in that one way. It wants to become a real boy.

"So," I say. "I should . . ."

"Yes!" she shouts. "Yes! All right!"

I jump up and search for my bathrobe in the blackness.

"Joe!" hisses Deb. "What are you doing? Get back here!"

"Nothing," I say, grabbing my bathrobe from the hook on the closet door. "I've got to go to the bathroom for a minute."

"Joe! Don't you dare!"

"I'm not. I swear. I've just got to . . ."

I open the door.

"Joe!"

I snap the door shut and sneak along the hallway toward the staircase. I feel like I have a high fever. My head is numb. This, I think, must be where the word *numbskull* comes from. My legs, like my skull, don't feel like they belong to me. Walking down the creaking stairs, wrapped in my green and white plaid bathrobe, my boner shrinking with every step, I realize that I am about to place myself in a precarious position. Because I have not mentioned word one of this to Kurt. I haven't even considered it. And I wouldn't have brought it up tonight if I hadn't been driven crazy by sex and the impending natural disaster. A sane man would know that the whole thing is much too seedy. No one wants to be the dude in a seventies porn video with the Fu Manchu and a perm. The swinger. It's gross.

Nonetheless, I reach the basement and find Kurt watching something on the Internet while reclining on the futon where Deb has made up his bed. He shoots me a suspicious look.

"Hey," he says, warily. He is unshaven.

"Hey," I say, taking a seat on the edge of the futon. "What you watching?"

Pause.

"I don't know," he says, relaxing a little. Crossing his feet at the ankles. "Some nature thing."

I nod. We both watch the nature thing. There is a mountain lion.

"Hey," I say, "maybe I'll stay down here for a while and watch this thing."

Pause.

"Yeah?"

"Yeah," I say, nodding, still looking at the screen. The mountain lion is walking around. "It looks pretty good."

"Just started," says Kurt.

"Deb's watching a movie in the bedroom," I say, avoiding eye contact.

Pause.

"Yeah?"

"Uh-huh."

Kurt is silent for another moment. I can't read his expression because I'm continuing to avoid eye contact. I'm staring hard at the lion, which is still walking around. There seems to be no plot at all to this nature thing.

"What movie she watching?" says Kurt, finally.

I turn and look at him. "I don't know," I say. "Some movie."

"Huh," says Kurt.

"Yeah," I say.

Now there are some other animals milling around near the river.

I turn and look at Kurt again. He is frowning.

"I don't know what it is," I say again, for no reason I can think of.

Kurt further intensifies his glare at the computer screen. "Well," he says, "I sort of want to see what happens on this thing."

Joe Blair

"Really?" I say.

"Yeah," he says. "This cougar . . . it's about to do something, I think."

I leave the basement and begin my ascent. The stairs creak loudly. My expansive libertine philosophies have withered and shrunken. I know without a doubt that there is something deeply wrong with me. How did I get myself into this situation? I have a feeling that it must be someone else's fault and the whole thing seems unfair in a way. Like I have been tricked into something.

You PAY ATTENTION WHEN you live on the floodplain. You think about the spillway. If the previous winter's snowfall was especially heavy, you think about the reservoir. You notice when the river is high. You pay attention when the thunderstorms come every day. This spring, the talk was all about the level in the reservoir.

"It's five feet from the top."

"It's three feet."

The National Guard has posted troops on either end of the Burlington Street Bridge as well as the Route 6 Bridge and the other two smaller bridges across the Iowa River. The river is already up to the girders on the Iowa Avenue Bridge. It's odd and exciting, the lack of traffic. The silent, surging river. It seems to be a very understated and courteous impending disaster. Dog's leash in one hand, my daughter's hand in the other, I watch the Iowa Avenue Bridge from the River Street side and wonder what will happen when the river brings all its force to bear against those girders in a way the engineers didn't necessarily plan on. D'Artagnan pulls at the leash. He is curious about everything and he wants to continue our walk. "Daddy," Lucy is saying. "Daddy. Daddy."

"Uh-huh?"

"If you could have a superpower, what would it be?" This is Lucy's question.

If we need to get downtown, I think, watching the water move beneath the bridge, we'll need to go out to Route 80 and take Dubuque . . . no. Dubuque is closed. We'll need to take Dodge Street . . .

"I'd fly," I say. "How about you?"

"I don't know," she says. "I guess I'd fly too."

"What's your favorite bird?" This is Lucy's next question.

I have responded to this question, from Sam and William, differently through the years. For a while I liked the meadowlark because the bird is such a contradiction, sitting all alone on the phone line as it always does, and looking so shaggy and disheveled with its fat belly and wing tips hanging down like an untucked shirt. But the song. Like a synthesized harmonica, something that cannot be duplicated by any other bird. I've always liked catbirds because they are gray and they have black caps and they do their best to mock other birds while their own call is so grating and, when I was a child, they would call and call over the blueberry marshes in our backyard. I like crows because everyone hates them. I like blue jays because Deb likes them. But, at the moment, I like barn swallows because they are a rainbow color and they look like ornamental kites and they fly like miracles and if I were a bird, I'd want to fly that way.

"Barn swallows," I say. "How about you?"

"I don't know," says Lucy. "I guess barn swallows."

When your daughter tells you she wants to make a birdhouse, what she means is, she wants you to sketch out the gable ends and the sidewalls and the roof pieces and the floor piece on a sheet of plywood and then cut the pieces on the table saw and then glue the pieces together and then let the glue set and then cut the hole for the bird to get in and then add a little dowel perch just beneath the hole. And then your daughter will take the birdhouse out to the backyard and paint it bright pink with flecks of yellow and orange and red and blue and green, like an electric disco party for Barbie dolls. And then she will present it to her mother and say, "Mommy, see the birdhouse I made?"

Lucy has a special little balcony on the east side of her bedroom. It's a quirk of house design that was necessitated by the sweeping, concave roof over the sunroom directly below. She has a four-by-five little place with a short knee wall where she has displayed little clay pots filled with flowers. Lucy opened her window and placed her disco birdhouse on the knee wall between the flowerpots. Looking at it from the neighbor's driveway, I could see, from that distant perspective, how the birdhouse was sort of higher than a normal birdhouse should be and more narrow with a too steeply pitched roof. Still, if ungainly, it was a cool-looking thing in a disco Barbie doll way.

"When do you think a bird will live there?" said Lucy, standing next to me in the neighbor's driveway. She is always impatient.

"I don't know," I said. "But a bird will live there. Wouldn't you want to live there?"

"It's a little bright," said Lucy.

That was last spring. No bird saw fit to live in Lucy's birdhouse. Not all summer long. Not a bluebird. Not a swallow. Not a sparrow. No bird.

There are reasons. Different birds, apparently, require different living situations. A chickadee, for instance, needs a hole that is one and one-eighth inches in diameter and that hole must be four to eight inches above the floor. There's even a certain width and depth and height that a chickadee requires. Apparently. According to the professional birdhouse builders that offer free birdhouse plans online. A titmouse, on the other hand, will not live anywhere other than a place where the hole is an inch and one-quarter in diameter. A western bluebird requires an inch and a half. And if you want to build a birdhouse that will suit a barn swallow, the most beautiful of all birds, you can't have a hole at all. What you need is simply a roof and a ledge.

Lucy is ten years old. She's been a little kid her whole life and there hasn't been much to worry about. But recently a seed of doubt has begun to grow.

"Someone said I was fat," Lucy said. This was last week. I was in my bedroom and she was in the bathroom down the hall. The door was closed, but I could still hear her voice.

"That's ridiculous," said Deb, incredulous. "Who said that?"

"I don't know," said Lucy.

"That's ridiculous. You're not fat at all. You're perfect." Deb hesitated. "What do you mean you don't know who said it?"

"It was a dream," said Lucy.

"What are you guys talking about?" I said, opening the bathroom door.

Deb was in the tub. Lucy was standing near the sink.

"Nothing," said Deb.

Of the twins, Lucy was born first. I was the first to hold her in my arms. Her entire body was bright red. "I think we should name her Scarlett,"

I told Deb. But Deb didn't answer. Because she wasn't done with Mike yet. Mike presented sideways. That's the way he wanted to come into the world.

"This isn't going to work," said the doctor.

"*What?*" shouted Deb. "What isn't going to work?"

"Hang in there, champ," said the doctor. The doctor called Deb champ. After the delivery, he called her a trouper. "You were a real trouper," he said.

Lucy likes to wrestle. "Want to wrestle, Dad?" she says. She asks almost every day after I come home from work. "Want to wrestle?" She always has a shtick when we wrestle. "Wait in there," she'll say, pointing to the living room. Then she'll circle through the dining room and make her entrance. She'll have the tablecloth wrapped around her neck like a cape and she'll say, "I'm Super Lucy!" Or she'll have a pillow stuffed under her shirt and she'll say, "I'm Strongman Lucy!" And then we'll wrestle on the throw rug, I on my knees and Lucy running around and around me until she finds an opening to attack.

Mike likes to wrestle too. I know this because he laughs when I wrestle with him. He generally doesn't ask to wrestle. He generally doesn't ask for anything. Generally, he listens to the strong sounds of crickets and the distant drums no one else can hear and the ringing of the neurons firing in his head. Mike has also been a kid his entire life. And worry seems to grip him from time to time as well. But he never mentions it to me the way Lucy does.

"Aaron Carter is going out with Zoe," says Lucy.

Joe Blair

We're lying in my bed now. It's seven o'clock in the morning. She has snuck in at some point during the night. I can't remember it. Deb is already up. She's giving Mike his bath.

"Chloe?" I say. "He's dating Chloe?"

"Not Chloe," she says. "*Zoe*. She's someone else."

"So they're dating?" I say.

"Well," she says. "Not really. We're only in elementary school."

"So they're not really dating?" I say.

"Well," she says. "They haven't kissed yet."

"How do you know?"

"Aaron told me, Dad!" she says. She sounds indignant.

"He told you?"

"Yes," she says.

"Okay," I say, after a while. "Get out of here. I've got to get ready for work."

Lucy doesn't want to go. She punches me in the arm.

"What's the matter?" she says. "Are you going to cry?"

"Come on, Lucy," I say. "I've got to get ready. Get out of here."

"What's the matter?" she says, trying to punch me again. When I grab her arm and use her own hand to hit her in the side of her head, she screams with laughter. She only wants to wrestle. But the world is calling. She knows it. She will need to pull on her low-rider jeans with bells and her new shirt.

"Like my new shirt?" she says, appearing in my bedroom doorway again.

"It looks like a swimsuit top," I say.

"It's not a swimsuit!" she says, insulted.

She is looking at herself in the large mirror mounted on the wall near my closet door. She shakes her curly hair. The hair everyone has always complimented her on.

"Somewhere," I once heard Deb tell her, "the boy you will marry is doing something right now. I don't know. Maybe he's brushing his teeth. But he's somewhere out there. You just don't know where yet. You know what we can do? Tonight, when we say our prayers? We can pray for him. That he'll be healthy and everything. So you'll be able to meet him."

Deb is finished bathing Mike, but he doesn't want to get out of the tub. I can tell because he begins to scream in that piercing, dog-whistle pitch. Deb will pull Mike out of the tub and dry him. Then she will pull on his sweatpants. (Sweatpants because there are no jeans that fit him—Mike being a little wide in the waist.) Then Deb will pull on his shirt. Maybe the "I'm a Naughty Monkey" shirt. Or the shirt that has the word *Football* on it. These are shirts that my older boys would never have worn at his age. By ten, they were wearing throwback Led Zeppelin and Pink Floyd T-shirts. There was already that distant call. Mike hears the call. It is a strong one. Soon it will be even stronger than the distant drums and the ringing. I've never heard Deb say anything about the girl Mike will marry. "Somewhere the girl you will marry is doing something right now." Because it isn't true. There is no girl Mike will marry. Deb or I will always wash Mike. Mostly, it's been Deb. In the bathtub or shower. Mike won't have a wife. One of us will always dress him in clothes he never would have chosen for himself if it weren't for the distant drums and the ringing and the crickets. And the approaching apocalypse of puberty. It will not be stopped. It will introduce desires and worries everyone knows will arrive but somehow no one has anticipated. "Somewhere the girl you will marry . . ."

Deb holds Mike's arm as we wait for the bus. I'm standing by the front walk wearing my navy blue heating-and-air-conditioning uniform with "Joe" stitched over the shirt pocket. Mike has his Space Chimps backpack slung over his shoulders. Deb has slung it there. Inside is his lunch. Something gluten- and casein-free like the doctor said. Something like celery and rice cakes. Things Michael never would have chosen to eat if he had a choice.

"Say good-bye to Daddy," says Deb, aiming Mike in my direction.

Mike looks at me. His eyes are liquid. There are drums sounding. He has forgotten why he is looking at me. But his mother is turning him. His mother wants something of him. "Say good-bye, Mike," she says.

"Good-bye, Mike," he says.

The old *Laugh-In* joke isn't funny anymore. It isn't a joke.

"Good-bye, Mike," I say, bringing him to me in a bear hug. Mike does not return my hug.

"See ya," says Lucy. She is tripping down the front stairs. She is carrying her scooter. She is wearing her low-rider jeans with bells. Aaron Carter is dating Zoe. But they're not really dating. They're not really dating because they're only in elementary school. But time is moving on and everyone is getting older. Which means that someday, Aaron Carter may be dating Zoe. Or maybe not. Who knows who he will date when he really dates someone?

I don't know the diameter of the hole I drilled in Lucy's birdhouse. I don't know how far that hole is from the floor of the birdhouse. I don't know whether or not birds care one way or the other about color. I'm thinking they probably do. Why else would so many of them be so vividly colored? They say it's to attract a mate. To bring something to them they do not already possess, if there can be such a thing. Something more than a brilliant song. More than physical beauty. More than the ability to fly. To swoop. To dive. More than all of this. To have someone come to you. To desire to make a home with you. To stay with you. To be your mate for life. To have children with you. To love you. Isn't that the way it's supposed to be?

"Why don't the birds want to live in my house?" Lucy asked me, near tears, as we stood in the neighbor's driveway, nearly a year after we had built it. "It's the color, isn't it? Do you think it's the color?"

"No, honey," I said. "It's not the color. I'm sure it's something I did."

DEB READ IN THE *Press-Citizen* that volunteer sandbaggers should bring work gloves and rubber boots, but she can't find any gloves in the house other than the yellow Playtex gloves she uses for doing the dishes, so she brings those. The closest thing she has to rubber boots are her faux L.L.Beans, so she pulls them on. The sky is heavy and there's a steady breeze from the west. The forecast calls for more thunderstorms. Deb likes rain. She always has. Still, apart from the childhood memory of her mother and the smell of soup, I can't help but believe it's not rain she loves, but being protected from it.

Lucy doesn't stop asking questions about sandbagging.

"Are we going to be in the river?" she says.

"No, honey," I say. "We're going to be *beside* the river."

"Can I go *in* the river?"

"No, honey."

"Why can't I go in the river?"

"The current is too strong," says Deb. "Besides, it's polluted."

"Why is it polluted?"

"I don't know. Runoff from the fields and stuff I guess."

"You don't know?"

"No, honey."

"Then how do you know it's polluted?"

"I've read about it, Lucy."

"Will there be other kids there?"

"I don't know."

"Can I dig in the sand?"

"I think so. I don't see why not."

"How much sand will there be?"

"Lucy, I've never done this before. It's my first time too."

"Will they let me help?"

"I'm sure they will, sweetheart."

Mike isn't so talkative. Deb believes that he is very smart. Mike, she maintains, has "an intelligence in his eyes." "He knows what's going on," she says. On the way down to Normandy Drive, Mike is holding Deb's hand and watching his feet very carefully as he walks. He might be thinking a thousand things.

"What if it rains again?" says Lucy.

"I don't know," I say.

"What if the river goes way up all of a sudden?"

"I don't know."

"Why are we going down there anyway?"

"We're going to help build a levee."

"What's that?"

"A wall. Out of sand."

"Why?"

"To stop the water."

"That won't work."

"Why do you say that?"

"Sand doesn't stop water."

"I think it does, honey. If it's in bags."

"I don't think it will," she says.

We know everyone down on Normandy Drive. We bought a split-entry on the street seven years ago. Sam and William were just starting school when we moved in. I needed to build a fence around the front yard so Mike could play outside. I started digging the postholes right along the driveway and I had already dug a few holes and poured the dry concrete and plumbed the posts when Deb told me that she wanted at least a foot between the driveway and the fence for her plantings. She wouldn't have a fence directly along her driveway. I managed to get the posts pulled out of the ground and I began to dig again, this time a foot back from the driveway like Deb wanted. She planted wildflowers. They grew high and crazy all along the fence. The Schirrocks and the Davises across the street hated them, Deb was sure. They never said anything, but she knew they hated them because their yards were perfectly neat and corporate-looking and their trees had circular brick borders around them with

Joe Blair

mulch, and their lawns had not one dandelion in them. Every week we'd
see the Quality Care truck pull up and spray their lawns with fertilizer
and broadleaf weed killer. Every spring, Quality Care would knock on our
door and offer us special deals, but Deb refused. We had four children
and Deb wouldn't have them running around barefoot and soaking up
poisonous chemicals. So, our yard was messy. "Like nature," said Deb.
With her crazy wildflowers and clover and dandelions and violets.

About a year ago, we sold the split-entry on Normandy and moved up
the hill to our current home, the pale yellow house on the corner of River
and Woolf. It's the kind of place you could imagine generations of family
members coming home to visit. With wives or husbands. Children.
Grandchildren. Built in 1908, it has what you might call a post-Mission
design with a sunken sunroom directly off the living room and a formal
dining room and a kitchen with solid, swinging doors. Cars appear
to wobble and weave as they pass by, the glass in the windows having
distorted over the years. The row of hundred-year-old pine trees along
River Street move in the wind as if underwater. It's a solid place. A place
that has lasted and has given every indication that it will continue to last.
A place to put down roots. To call your own. You could even name it, if
you were that sort of person. Maybe you could call it The Pines.

I dug the postholes for the new picket fence by hand, just like I had done at
the previous place down on Normandy, and cut each picket with my chop
saw. I spent days peeling the tar paper off the kitchen floor to reveal the
yellow pine boards beneath. I replaced the furnace myself. And I replaced
every sink and toilet as well as most of the lighting fixtures. We paid
for a new roof. I dug up the walk out front and found, about five inches
down, a second walk that must have been the original, laid when horses
and buggies rattled by. The coal delivery truck visited this house during

the early 1900s. The milkman. The iceman. Generations of paperboys. The pale yellow house on the corner is more than a house, really. It's a residence. It's an address. Built by Dr. O'Brien, the chief ophthalmologist at the University of Iowa, just before World War I. After we signed the papers, we were handed the original blueprints for the place. Little notes here and there describing what kind of wood floor to use (yellow pine in the kitchen; red oak everywhere else) or details regarding the eaves. Simply by signing a few papers, we had purchased, as we saw it, one hundred years of history. I had visions of living and dying in the pale yellow house. Of my children's children mowing the yard. And the idea was appealing for a while. Deb had me add a small, quirky second gate at the rear of the property, explaining that when her sister got married, and we had the ceremony out in what would someday be "the garden," the bride needed a place to make her entrance. Sort of a *surprise* entrance, she imagined, and all the guests would simultaneously turn and, all at once, let out a collective sound of appreciation.

Every influence in our lives—our parents, the movies we watched, the books we read—led us to believe that this, this idea of ownership of a house, was of unquestionable importance. So, one day, we bought the house. And after that day, during each hour of every weekend, if I'm not cleaning my gutters or sweeping my walks or mowing my lawn or shoveling my driveway or painting my trim or repairing my chimney or painting my basement floor or renovating my bathroom or hanging cabinets or replacing windows, I'm feeling guilty that I'm not doing more to maintain the house. Why? Because it's our house. And it has lasted a hundred years so far. And its previous owners kept it in good condition. And what would it say about us if we were to let it go? Let the roof grow moss? Let the driveway crack? And the pine trees go untrimmed? And the ground squirrels dig holes beneath the foundation? What kind of guy doesn't care for his house? While his children attempt to sneak off to visit their friends.

Joe Blair

We have many fights about chores, my children and I. I shout quite a bit.
I figure I need to teach those kids how to do the very thing I hate to do:
maintain a house. We can't have them running off without first taking
out the trash. Or sorting the recyclables. Or bringing in firewood. Or at
least cleaning their rooms. Who would think there'd be so many chores?
Who would think there'd be so much shouting on my part and so much
slacking off on the kids' part? Deb cleans. The wood floors need a certain
type of oil-based cleaner. Four toilets in that house. Seven sinks. Three
showers. Four bedrooms. Deb cleans. She also picked out new colors for
everything. And not just once. We had the kitchen painted twice. The first
time in Kermit the Frog green. The second in seafoam. It is crucial, she
believes, that we live surrounded by certain colors. Vibrant colors like in
the movies. But not so vibrant that our color choices decrease the value
of the house if we ever did choose to sell. Even though we never will
sell. How could we sell such a beautiful house? A residence. An address.
Where the children's children will mow the lawn.

About fifty years before the house was built, Henry David Thoreau,
that strange man who mooched off his rich friends and relations and did
nothing but sit around in a cabin and write essays and books that are still
in print, asked the fundamental question, Does the man own the farm,
or does the farm own the man? It's a rhetorical question. He only put it
in the form of a question because he didn't want to sound overly shrill
or admonishing by writing a declarative statement like "Owning a house
sucks! Besides, ownership is an illusion. There will be floods."

ALONG NORMANDY DRIVE, the heavy equipment has already churned up the lawns everyone was so proud of. The ground is soft from all the rain and the dump trucks and earthmovers have destroyed the grass, leaving deep scars. Tommy Turner stands on the street inspecting his destroyed lawn. We know how much he loves things to be orderly. Deb might argue that, in one way, this chaos could be seen as a victory for nature.

"I'm so sorry, Tom," says Deb.

He smiles. "Oh," he says, "it don't matter. Important thing is we're all doing what we can. Thanks for coming down to help, sweetheart."

I feel my nose start to burn and I know tears will come if I don't think about something practical.

"Where do you need us?" I say.

"Oh," he says, "I saw a lot of sandbaggers down there near the end of the road."

"Thanks," says Deb and gives him a hug. He looks nervous about the hug.

We walk down Normandy in the direction Mr. Turner had pointed. William's math teacher, a big, tough-looking guy, seems to be in charge of this phase of the operation. "Where do you need us?" I say.

"Bagging," he says. "But you won't want to wear those." He juts out his chin at my new steel-toed Red Wing work boots.

"Why not?" I say.

Again he juts out his chin, this time toward the river. A line of twenty or so people are passing sandbags one to the next. Some are already waist deep in the rising water. "Ruin 'em," he says.

"We need someone here!" shouts a man from the river.

"I thought you said we weren't going in the river," says Lucy.

"I guess Daddy was wrong," says Deb.

"What are they doing?" Lucy asks.

"Building a levee," says Deb.

"Can I go in?"

"We can't let kids go in there," says William's math teacher.

"Where can the kids help?" I ask.

He points in the same direction we have just come from. "They're filling bags down there," he says. "Kids usually tie 'em up with the stuff. The twine. But we could use you right here. We're kind of stretched on the line."

"Lucy," says Deb, turning to Lucy, who is pouting, "take Mike down there and fill bags."

"I can't fill bags with Michael there!" she shouts. "It's not fair!"

"Get one of the boys," says Deb, turning toward the water, "and tell them to take Mike home."

"*How am I going to find the boys?*" she shouts, almost hysterical now.

"We could use someone right here!" shouts a woman from the river.

"Lucy," says Deb, sensing the urgency of the sandbaggers, "we've got to help right now. Can you please help me out? Here"—she's handing Lucy her cell phone—"you can call them on this. Keep it. I can't take it in the water." Lucy snatches the phone from Deb's hand and starts trying to drag Michael away from the river. Michael doesn't want to move and he begins screaming and throwing a temper tantrum. Deb needs to help Lucy get Michael to the street. She snatches her phone back from Lucy.

"I'll do it," says Lucy.

"*I'll* do it," says Deb.

"Here," I say, handing Deb my phone. "Can you take this? Thanks." And I head for the river.

Deb gives me a dry look that stops me.

"What?" I say. "Okay. Let me do it. I'll do it. You go."

Deb hands me both phones and walks toward the river. After about a half an hour, I settle the Michael problem. "Don't leave him alone!" I tell William, who has walked down from the other side of the neighborhood, where he was bagging sand.

"I know, Dad," he says.

"Not even for a second."

"Dad," says William. "I know. How long you going to be?"

"I don't know," I say. "Just don't—"

"I know," says William, pulling Michael by the hand.

I hesitate, looking at my new Red Wings, and then I wade into the swollen, brown water of the Iowa River. Deb, who is completely covered in mud, looks like she's been working all day. "You got it?" she says, after we've finished unloading sandbags from the bed of a black E-250 pickup truck. The empty truck pulls away, wheels spinning in the mud.

"Yeah," I say. "William came down."

Deb smiles. She's happy here in the water. "Thanks," she says.

I begin my sandbagging career on the bottom rung. I don't feel too bad about it because, as I quickly discover, there is only one rung. The first bag is wet and heavy. Maybe forty pounds. I receive the bag from a tall guy with a beard, turn, and pass it to a woman wearing a Milwaukee Brewers baseball cap. The tall guy with the beard passes me another bag. I turn and pass to the woman in the baseball cap. Passing sandbags is a personal thing. You're face-to-face with the person passing you the bag, as well as the person to whom you pass the bag. The line may be three hundred feet long. But it's not long for each individual. It's an intimate thing. A three-person activity. You take. You turn. You give. There is no doubt it's personal. And you get to know people. Not through conversation. But by the way they hand you the bag. The way they work. On some levels, it's a better relationship than any other I've had. There's no second-guessing. No petty games. The person receiving the bag doesn't need to ask you to receive it and the person giving you the bag doesn't expect anything in return. And then, the sad part, the heartbreaking part in a way, is when the latest pickup truck pulls away and your little threesome breaks up, the line disintegrating and then re-forming for the next load. Sometimes you get the same partners. But most of the time you get new partners. Sometimes the new partners are stronger or more efficient than the old ones. Sometimes weaker and less efficient. And on you go. Working. Sweating. Manual labor is the best thing. Whatever reason you might have to do the work fades after a while because you're working as hard as you can and it's fun.

No one speaks much. Even when we have a break between loads. We wade out of the water. Some stretch. Some fall on the ground, arms wide, like little children, and relax completely. I try to make conversation. "They were supposed to be good this year," I say to the woman in the Brewers hat. She frowns. I motion toward her hat. "Oh," she says. "It's not my hat." And then she walks away.

It's late afternoon when Deb decides to quit sandbagging. She wades over to where I'm working and gives me a lingering kiss. I know I haven't done anything to deserve it. Matter of fact, I feel guilty about it. But there's no time to think about that now. Who has time to think? I'm working. I don't have time to think about anything. Deb wades back to shore and begins her walk up the hill to our pale yellow house. I receive a sandbag. I pass the sandbag on. I receive a sandbag. I pass the sandbag on.

My head is completely clear now. Those grotesque and shameful demons that crowded around in the dark of night and in the midst of sex and alcoholic stupor have fled. I don't think they were even real. In fact, I'm sure they were not. I understand things now. In a simple way. In a simple and good and pure way. I'm certain now. Absolutely certain. I receive a sandbag. I pass the sandbag on. I'm doing a good thing. I'm building a levee. Because I'm a good person. I'm a hero. I'm helping to save the neighborhood. Look at me receive the sandbag! Look at me pass the sandbag on!

About an hour later, Deb reappears on the water's edge. She has brought Mike down to the river. "Hey!" I say, wading out of the river. "Hey, Mike!

Joe Blair

Oh, look! Thanks!" I say, when I notice she's carrying a picnic basket in her right hand.

"You got a call," she says.

"Really?" I say.

I make a grab for the basket. Deb pulls it away. This is not like sandbagging at all.

"Who's Joe?" she says.

I know I should have had someone in mind for this moment. Some explanation to throw out.

But, "Oh," I say. "Just a guy."

"What guy?"

"Over at the rest home. What's its name? Greenwood Manor?"

"I thought that was Jay."

"Yeah," I say. "It is. Joe is . . . Jay's helper." I grab for the basket again, but Deb takes a step back.

"You know," she says, "I felt bad for resenting you earlier. When I had to go home and you stayed to work?"

"I told you I'd go," I say.

"Both of us knew I'd be the one," she says. "But that's not important. Like I said, I felt guilty about that. I was just remembering the time you moved that fence back for me. Remember that? You moved that fence back so I could plant my flowers? You did that for me. And I was thinking about that. And I was thinking how you were a good man and a good husband, too. And that's why I made this." She holds up the basket and gives it a wiggle. "And then, on the way down, I was thinking about how you always wanted me to clean up those toys around the yard and I never did? And I felt bad about that, and I thought, Why didn't I clean those up?"

"Yeah?" I say.

"And then your phone rang," she says. "And it showed up as Joe. But the funny thing is, when I answered, Joe hung up. Why do you think he'd do that?"

"I don't know," I say. "Why don't you call him back?"

"I did," she says. "And you know what's funny? He didn't answer."

"Hm," I say. "Well, some guys are strange. You know? I know it's wrong, but some of my customers, they feel uncomfortable talking to women."

"Yeah," she says. "That is strange. But, if I called back on your phone, wouldn't he assume it was you?"

"I don't know, Deb!" I say. "I'm not a frigging mind reader! Look, am I on trial here? Would you mind if I just looked in that basket for a minute?"

"You know," she says, "that Peter thing? That was nothing. I'm not calling Peter on the phone. And if he called me, I would tell him not to. I'd feel like that was being unfaithful to you."

"Deb," I say. "Could you please not talk so loud?"

"And now you get these phone calls, and I know it's a woman. I know it is."

"No it's not," I say.

"It is," she says. "And you're a liar. *I'm* not a liar. You are." She takes a deep breath, as if she's about to go underwater. "You know something, Joe Blair?" she says, exhaling. "You're one hundred percent unauthentic. You're unauthentic. You're not even real. You're . . . nothing."

"Yes, I am," I say. "I'm . . . something."

Joe Blair

Deb places the picnic basket on the ground, grabs Mike by the hand, and pulls him in the direction of the house.

By nine o'clock at night, when the sun has swollen into a large red blob, and it's cool, and the sandbaggers are wandering off to wherever it is they came from, I know that I have participated in something good. I chat with some of my old neighbors as I walk toward the hill. Everyone is hugging and shaking hands. We are proud of ourselves. Louise Novak, whose boiler I had installed a year and a half ago at Christmastime, hugs me and thanks me for helping save the old neighborhood.

I'M TAKING D'ART FOR A WALK!" I shout to the quiet house. No one answers. The kids are probably asleep. And Deb's not speaking to me anyway.

I leave through the garage. D'Artagnan leaps with joy. We head down the hill on Lee Street toward the place where we built the levee earlier in the day. We walk down along Rocky Shore, where the water has found a way to circumnavigate the levee, just like the Persians did at Thermopylae, and river water is now bubbling up through the storm drains. When I see Pamela's hunter green Subaru Outback clear the crest of the hill, my heart races. She parks the car, jumps out, and runs toward me. We embrace and then we kiss. There is no reservation in us and we withhold nothing and it's like releasing a deep sigh, to kiss someone without reservation. "I love you," I say. "I love you too," she says. And it seems to mean something. She is, I'm sure now, all that I have wanted. Everything I have waited for. We can't stop embracing here in the dark, on Rocky Shore. There is no sound other than the ready-power pumps down near the levee. There is no light but the moon. She's holding me fiercely, her breasts pressing low against my chest, her hand warm, now, on my face. I return the pressure, keeping one arm free to continually yank the dog back when he tries to run out over the purple landscape. Under the moon. Beside the water. And into the water. All of the things d'Artagnan could do if he were free! All of the places he could run!

Pamela and I hold hands as we walk. Pamela's hands are larger than Deb's. Her shoulders are broader. She is different. We stop walking when we reach the river. There is darkness and the sound of the river. When we kiss again with a passion I believed I had lost the ability to possess. A passion verging on desperation. We embrace and kiss one another until we are exhausted. And still we embrace and kiss one another.

Eventually, Pamela and I separate and stand in the darkness by the rising river. Before too long, a guy on a bike coasts to a stop beside us. I recognize him as the tall dude with the beard who had been my partner more than once on the sandbagging line the previous day. He removes his helmet and we stand and look at the river. After a few moments, someone else is at our side. I recognize him too. He was the guy who set up his iPod dock and played Howlin' Wolf and Muddy Waters all day long. We all stand together, looking out. "It's a nice wall we built," says the guy with the iPod dock. We nod.

T HE FOLLOWING DAY, the water crests a few feet over our sandbag levee down on Normandy Drive and all the houses go under. The Shirrocks' and the Davises'. Our old house. The house on the peninsula. All the other houses. They are all filled with brown river water—silently, kindly, almost lovingly—right up to the ceilings of the first floors.

Nine thousand people are evacuated from their homes in Cedar Rapids. One hundred seventy patients are moved from Mercy Hospital, which is on Eighth Street, about a mile from the river. More than one thousand city blocks are underwater. The Cedar River, they say, will crest at seventeen feet over flood stage, which will break, by twelve feet, the record set in 1851. In Iowa City, six hundred homes have been evacuated and fifteen university buildings have been flooded. Two million acres of soybeans and one point three million acres of corn in the state of Iowa, or about 12 percent of the entire crop, are underwater. Heavy thunderstorms are predicted throughout the weekend. It is also predicted that the rivers haven't peaked yet.

Part Three

IN HIS LATER YEARS, when listing his accomplishments he was most proud of, Sir Isaac Newton put *celibacy* at the top of his list. If we can take him at his word (and I don't see why we can't), Sir Isaac Newton had never been laid. And he was proud of it. To be more proud of one's resistance to physical passion than, say, *discovering the laws of motion . . .* that says something. What it says, I think, is that what a man refrains from defines him perhaps more clearly than what he accomplishes.

Pamela runs through the darkness behind the Sycamore movie theater to my van. She's smiling as she crosses her arms and leans against my open window. "Hi," she says, glowing.

"Hi," I say. I'm glowing too. "You parked crooked."

She glances at her little car, then back at me. "Excited girl," she says.

She climbs into my van and we park on a dark street somewhere near the theaters. We make out like high school kids. One guy turns on his porch light and we hunker down in our seats, afraid of getting caught. Maybe the guy saw us making out. Maybe he's going to call the cops. But he isn't calling the cops. He's feeding his dogs. We giggle. After the guy goes back inside, we jump out of the van and walk around the dark, working-class neighborhood. We hold hands and swat bugs and comment on different houses we see. There's one with vines covering the windows. There's a little ranch with huge pillars holding up the tiny little roof over the front stoop. How silly that is! The warm weather has come. With all the rain, everything is junglelike. Growing furiously. Madly. And then, back in the van again, Pamela talks about Brussels. And wine. And art. And I want all of these things. And I want her. I believe that love is enormous. Too large for any two people. Capable of encompassing everyone on earth. I believe I might love everyone. And I'm kissing Pamela again and feeling her soft skin.

A tornado will tear a building apart, which isn't a good thing. But at least it's easy to understand. "My home," says the victim, wading through the rubble, "has been completely destroyed."

Fire has the grace to relieve a structure of the very materials that allow it to exist.

But a flood works differently. A flood infects a building with itself and leaves it standing, to rot and fester and steal away hope from those who venture inside.

Scenes flash through my mind, unbidden. Things that were and never will be again. Even as I lie sprawled over the console of my GMC Sierra, Pamela's breasts bare, my head uncomfortably perched on her shoulder, I think of the Honda ST1100 whirring along a brushy dirt road north of Quebec, Deb's hands shoved in the pockets of my leather coat. I think of the time, in the Midwest, when we stopped on an old service road that ran parallel to the highway. Small trees growing all along the shoulders. The road had been abandoned. It was completely unused. The little town had a water tower and a Dairy Queen and a few houses and nothing else. Narrow roads dead-ended in cornfields. And Deb climbed off the bike and sat right in the middle of that road. Right where the faded lines ran. And the weeds growing up. Long hair braided and slung over one shoulder. Goggles slung around her neck. Levi's turned up at the cuffs and a cotton shirt from, I think, Goodwill. And the black cowboy boots I bought her instead of an engagement ring. She called them her engagement boots. We figured a wedding ring was good enough.

I look at my finger. I'm still wearing my ring, Deb's name engraved inside. Pamela talks about Europe. I tell her I've never been. "Oh," she says. Then she tells me about some Piazza del Duomo or other. And the Louvre. And what it's like in the Netherlands. She wants to show me the world. "You'd love it in Europe," she says. She wants to introduce me to a certain kind of red wine. All of this sounds capital. Just capital. But I wonder how I'll make money so I can send it to my family. I can't see myself hanging out in Valencia when the mortgage is due. "You've got to see Paris! *Everyone* has to see Paris!"

Bottles of liquor float on the surface of the water down on the Coralville Strip. They keep showing it on the news. They show an overweight woman wading through the water and retrieving as many of them as she can carry. Speedboats are tearing up the beautiful surface of the water in Cedar Rapids, their rooster tails drenching the front entrance to the library. Everything is free at Hosier Refrigeration Supply on Eighth Avenue. Yellow plastic boxes containing things like electrical meters and pneumatic controls float all around. It is like an overpowering dream. It has nothing to do with cultural advancement. Or philosophic enlightenment. Or scientific revolution. It is much lower than that. More base. And much more powerful. So powerful, in fact, that it cannot be stopped. Restraint is not what people want in a time of flood. We are attracted to the undertow of passion, so akin to the base sensations of fear or hunger that it almost cannot be distinguished from them. We want to want. We want, also, to be wanted. And when we want another person with that strong and ancient urge and when that other person wants us, what can it be but love? The lowest form of love. Exclusive to us. Excluding all others. We want to be rained upon by it. To be flooded with it. To be dragged out to sea by it. We want a passionate type of love. A fearful love. A hungry love. Jealous and violent. The sort of love a mob has for destruction.

A T FIRST, I CAN'T make out what it is. Skin. There is definitely skin. And there is also hair. Not hair-on-the-head hair. But hair. Probably pubic. And something that looks like a hand. And a knee. There is definitely something erotic about it. After a few moments, everything snaps into place. She is lying on her back. And touching herself with one hand, one leg bent, knee facing the ceiling.

"I have something for you," Pamela had told me breathlessly over the phone.

"Okay," I said, adjusting my wrench to fit the half-inch bolt on the compressor mount.

"Can I drop it off to you?" she said.

"I don't know," I said. "I'm working."

"Where?"

"Um," I said, "over at the IRP?"

"What's the IRP?"

"The Iowa River Power Restaurant? On First Avenue in Coralville?"

"I know where it is," she said. "I'll be there in twenty minutes."

Joe Blair

And she hung up.

When she pulled into the parking lot, Ben, an enormous ex–Coe College football player who was a cook before the flood closed the restaurant, and Jim, an ex–Golden Gloves boxing champion who was a kitchen manager, were looking for the hundred-dollar bill that the crane operator had dropped while removing the ruined HVAC equipment and lowering the new equipment into place.

"It must have fallen out of my pocket when I pulled my keys out or something," the crane operator had said over the phone. "I don't know. I had it. And now I don't have it."

"We haven't seen it," I told him, "but . . . we'll definitely look around."

I approached Pamela Bell's hunter green Subaru while Jim and Ben hunted for the money.

"Hi," I said, bending down and peering at her through the passenger-side window.

"Hi," she said, handing me the envelope. "Come over this side."

"What's up?" I said, standing my ground, glancing back at Jim.

"I just want to kiss you," she said. "Come here."

I leaned in through the passenger-side window and she leaned over across the stick shift and we kissed briefly.

"I love you," she said, still leaning.

"Thanks," I said, straightening.

She gave me an air kiss and a fairy-dust wave and then she drove away.

I am well aware that the photograph I hold in my hand, even though it is at first almost impossible to make out, is very dangerous. I know that I should throw it into the Dumpster along with the wet duct insulation and molding carpet and four-foot chunks of muddy drywall that Jim and Ben have hauled out of the flood-ravaged restaurant. But I don't. I stick the kryptonite thing in my glove compartment. It doesn't thrill me, the photograph. It frightens me. The photograph, or more precisely Pamela's delivery of the photograph, makes it clear to me what, exactly, is going on: nothing will ever be a secret. I am not safe at work. This woman, Pamela Bell, is more than willing to cross the work/not work boundary. And if she can cross that boundary, she can cross the home/not home boundary. She is not a woman who will allow herself to be relegated or hidden. She will be out. Like the truth.

"Who was that?" says Jim as I wander back in his direction.

"Some woman," I say.

"Where would I go," says Ben in a singsong voice, scanning the destroyed fryers and stovetops and reach-in coolers, "if I were a hundred-dollar bill?"

"I saw that," says Jim. "But who is she?"

"I have no fucking idea," I say.

Jim crosses his muscular arms over his barrel chest and grins.

Ben, bending at the waist, walks slowly among the destroyed barstools and waffle irons and wooden tables. The wind is strong and I know that the hundred-dollar bill is probably in the river by now.

"You're fucking her," says Jim.

"No," I say. "I'm not. I'm not *fucking* her . . ."

Joe Blair

"But you *fucked* her."

"Sort of."

"How do you *sort of* fuck someone?"

"It's difficult."

"What'd she give you?"

"What do you mean?"

"Just now. What'd she give you?"

"A picture of her playing with herself."

Jim lets out a loud, single burst of laughter. "No."

"Yes."

"Let me see it."

"No."

"You won't let me see it?"

"No."

"Good," he says, uncrossing his arms. "I don't want to see it anyway." He has enormous, pale blue eyes with deep black lashes and a sweet smile, like a child. These things, along with the tree-trunk neck and the crew cut and the five-day growth and the deep scar on his forehead, make him look like a beautiful murderer.

"That's good then," I say.

Jim shakes his head and glances around low, looking for the money. "That's sort of fucked up," he says.

"What is?"

"That is."

"Yeah."

"She's crazy," he says, still scanning the ground.

"Yeah," I say. I glance at Ben, who is now on his hands and knees. "Like a fox."

"Ha! Well," says Jim, "better not let the old lady find out."

"Probably too late," I say.

Jim studies me, big arms still crossed. I look out over the destroyed parking lot. A blue Ford Taurus, all four tires flat, interior filled with silt, is parked at an angle near the chain-link fence that encircles the power transfer station next door.

"That's too bad," he says, finally.

"Yeah," I say.

"Hey!" shouts Ben, holding something up in the air. "I found it!"

Jim and I swivel our heads in his direction. Ben is beaming, his huge, Baby Huey arms uplifted.

"A hundred bucks!" he shouts. He unfolds the hundred-dollar bill, which has been folded neatly twice. "That's a hundred beers," he says with glee.

"You know we've got to give it back to that kid," I say. "He's a good kid."

A shadow passes over Ben's face. "I ain't calling that kid."

"You got to," I say. "I'll call him. I'll tell him he's got to bring a six-pack when he picks it up. What do you drink?"

"Bud," says Ben, massive shoulders slumping.

"I'll tell him," I say.

"A twelve-pack," says Ben. "Tell him a twelve-pack."

"Okay," I say, phone already to my ear. "I'll tell him."

After I call the kid, we all begin to make our way back inside. The three big walk-in coolers in the basement, all of which are loaded with rotten food, need to be emptied and removed. All of the ice machines need to be thrown out. Everything is still coated with brown sludge. The old fifteen-horsepower sump pump, the one that failed, needs to be rebuilt.

"Shit," says Ben. "Why am I such a good guy?"

"Don't know," says Jim.

THERE IS AN ATMOSPHERE, all around the flooded city, of irresistible change. All of the activities we thought were inevitable—our commutes to work, our trips to the grocery store—are now impossible. And many things we thought would never happen are in the process of happening.

My fourteen-year-old son, William, and I paddle our canoe through the old neighborhood. We paddle through what used to be City Park and has now become a part of the river. We aren't supposed to take the canoe through the neighborhood. But we do it anyway. Over the four-foot picket fence I had built in our old front yard, where Deb had planted her wildflowers. Over driveways and mailboxes. It's a far more beautiful neighborhood now than it has ever been before, half submerged in water like it is.

"I was okay," Louise Novak said after she and her family had been evacuated from their home, "but then I saw the boiler you installed. It was my Christmas present that year, you know. We decorated it with Christmas lights and bulbs. When I saw that, I cried."

Joe Blair

I wait for e-mails from Pamela. Little missives from that other world. Like the tiny notes kids pass from one to another in middle school. Written in miniature, cramped sentences in smudged ink on corners of notebook paper ripped in tiny rectangles.

Most of the e-mails I get are MLB fantasy updates and notices regarding Facebook comments. I don't open these e-mails. I delete them and then I go to Facebook and see who is saying what. I won't usually comment because I hate it when my wall gets filled up with people saying things like "Go Hawks!" Then I go back to my e-mail again. Because you never know. Something might have come in while I was on Facebook. It's pathetic, how badly I want some kind of correspondence. But the truth is, even when I do get an e-mail from Pamela, and even when it's quite personal, like "I was just thinking about you. Are you okay?" Or "Joe, I love you. I need to see you. Where have you been today? When can we meet?" And even when I respond, when I tell Pamela that I love her too and I can meet at two o'clock today, it's not enough. It's never enough.

There must be some higher calculus that will solve the question of my infidelity. Even when I'm with Deb and we're in the middle of sex, during that time of insanity when I say things I don't mean and do things I'll later cringe at the memory of, I wonder why, in God's name, this can't be enough for me. For us. Can't this be enough?

"I cannot write with you anymore." This was the first part of the e-mail I sent to Pamela two weeks ago, before we met at the river. "And I can't tell you why. It just cannot be. I had a dream about you tonight. You were wearing that green shirt."

That last part about the green shirt was a lie. In fact, I didn't have any dreams that night. Any I could recall.

Later that same morning, I got my reply: "Wha?" Just that. Misspelled like that.

I didn't respond.

Eventually, Pamela e-mailed again: "I don't understand your last email. You were the one who wanted to write together in the first place and of course if you don't want to meet again that's fine, but I'd like to understand why that might be."

I e-mailed back something less cryptic like "I don't think it's a good idea for me to spend time with you because I'm married" (I should have ended it right there. But I couldn't) "and you're beautiful."

I'm ashamed of myself for writing this response in the first place and now I'm ashamed again for recalling it. Such obvious hypocrisy. Such unoriginal, heavy-handed schlock. It seems I can't even cheat on my wife with a hint of originality or integrity. I might as well have written "My wife doesn't understand me!"

Pamela pretended to be shocked by my declaration of her beauty. She pretended not to think of me. And to be unaware that I had begun to think of her when I was alone. And when I was with Deb. But this was an act. We knew what game we were playing. The false shock on her part and the lies on my part, however, were justified when we met down at Terrapin for the "final time" and I confessed to her the reason I needed to stop writing with her. "I think I might be falling in love with you," I said.

"That's why. That's why we probably shouldn't be . . . you know . . ." She nodded. And shortly thereafter, she excused herself and drove away in her little green car. Then, a day later, I received a tender e-mail that began "That was quite a bombshell you dropped yesterday . . ." and contained a poem by Rilke as an attachment.

Tonight, it's an elegiac poem by Keats. I've just opened the attachment when I hear a sound on the stairway and quickly clear the screen.

"Joe," says Deb, turning the corner from the stairway. "Joe. Joe."

She's speaking darkly, in a tone I have been conditioned to fear.

"Yeah?" I say.

Deb is holding my cell phone in front of her like it's a Geiger counter. "You got a call from Joe again."

"Really?" I say. "What . . . did . . . he say?"

"*He*," she says the word skeptically, "hung up."

"Really?" I say. "Hmm."

"Who's Joe?"

"Um . . . that guy. I already told you."

"Oh," she says. "Must be a real emergency. At this hour."

"Yeah," I say.

"When I called him back," says Deb, "he didn't answer. Again."

"Really?" I say. "Hmm."

I wait, but Deb doesn't say anything else. She doesn't even look especially angry. She simply turns and walks up the stairs. I sit at the computer for a few minutes. Then, after a beat or two, I exit my account. And then I follow her upstairs.

Since the flood, it has occurred to me that there is no safe place to be. And whatever bird we might choose as our *favorite* bird, whatever superpower we wished to possess when we were children; whatever pictures we might have drawn—this one of a man running; this one of a comic book character—whatever little things that have come to us and then come from us will be washed away by time. Deb was right. I am nothing. All of the times I have mown that lawn. All of the times I have painted the house. All of the payments I have made. All of the snow I have shoveled. All the times I trimmed the hedge. Like all of the times I said "I love you" and "I love you" and "I love you." None of it was mine. None of it belonged to me. It could all be washed away.

Deb isn't reading when I turn the corner into our room; she's only pretending to read. I take a seat on the very edge of the bed.

Deb closes her book and removes her reading glasses. "So," she says after a long pause, "I'm going to do this my new way. I'm not going to be the way I was. I'm different now."

"Really?" I say.

"Yes," she says. "I'm reading a book on black-and-white thinking. It's very interesting. And I sort of recognize myself."

"Uh-huh."

"And I went to an AA meeting. Did you know that? And . . . I'm thinking of becoming a Buddhist."

"Oh," I say. "That's cool."

Joe Blair

"Anyway," she says. "So, is Joe a woman?"

I sigh. "Yes," I say.

"Is Joe Pamela Bell?" she says.

"Yes," I say.

My hands are folded on my lap. I am waiting.

"I checked the number," she says. "I know that's who you called all those times."

"That's right," I say.

"And I've read your e-mails. I'm sorry. But you left them open and I read them."

"Uh-huh."

"Are you in love with her?" she says.

"I don't know," I say. "I think I am."

Deb nods. "Are you willing to give her up?"

"No," I say. "I don't think so."

Things have changed now. Not in the slow, revolving way planets spin— but quickly and violently, the way all things began. This is what the truth will do.

Deb has angry red rashes on her chest and face. She is breathing raggedly. Not crying, though. "So," she says thickly. "This is really it."

"I think so," I say.

"What do you mean you think so? What does that mean?"

"I'm sorry," I say. "I didn't mean to do it this way. I got . . . confused."

"You fell in love."

"Yeah," I say. "I guess I did."

THE LIGHT IS UNSURE of itself. The shadows are long and thin. Something about the morning makes the birds want to sing. I'd like to believe there is a reason for it—all the singing. Eventually, the light finds its feet and the wind comes up and the birds go about accomplishing useful things.

Deb left early this morning. She said she had an appointment with a lawyer and then a real estate agent. She's not messing around. She's taking the ball and running with it. I, on the other hand, am sitting at the kitchen table. I'm studying the tabletop up close. It used to be white. Until Deb painted it black. Then, she changed her mind about the color and started to scrape the black paint off with a wire brush. And then she changed her mind again. There are scrape marks all over the tabletop. Deb says it's okay. She calls it shabby chic.

"Somewhere Only We Know" is on. "Oh, simple thing," it goes, "where have you gone?" Sam and William are hidden away in the recesses of the house. Probably playing Grand Theft Auto Three. Or Four. Or whatever. Mike is pacing back and forth over his patch of dirt in the backyard. I'm staring at the black kitchen table that used to be white. "I'm getting old and I need something to rely on," the song goes. Time is moving slowly.

Joe Blair

We have the entire summer. The whole summer is ahead of us. "So tell me when you're gonna let me in. I'm getting tired and I need somewhere to begin." Time is slow. It moves so slowly. But I know that time is tricky. It fools you. It's slow, yes. But it's fast too. And soon, the summer will be gone. The county fairs. The state fair. Cows and horses on display. The prize hog with nuts the size of small pumpkins. Sweet corn and swimming pools. Time is tricky. "And if you have a minute, why don't we go talk about it somewhere only we know?" I've wasted it. I believe that. It's too late. I'm too late. "This could be the end of everything. So why don't we go somewhere only we know?" I've gotten it wrong. I've been wrong. I've been wrong. I believe that. And it's too late.

I don't jump when I feel the warm hand on my shoulder. The touch is steady and reassuring. I don't even wonder who it might be. I know it's Michael. My son. I don't look up. I'm leaning my weight on my elbows, my face hidden in the cradle of my forearms. Mike keeps his hand on my shoulder and then, slowly, he places his other hand on my other shoulder and lowers his face so that his cheek is touching my ear. And he stays like this through "Somewhere Only We Know," and through the next song. Mike's chest is pressed against my back, his hands are on my shoulders. No tremors. No giggles or shouts. My son stays with me like this. This is how he loves me.

After I pull myself together, I try to give Mike a hug, but he's having none of it. He pushes me away, shouting.

"Oh yeah?" I say. "I know you want to hug me!" And I advance on him.

Smiling slightly, he shuffles away into the living room.

"Come here!" I shout, in hot pursuit. "Come here!"

Mike falls backward over the arm of the couch and brings his knees up to his chin.

"Come on," I say, grabbing his hands. "I'll help you up! Don't worry, pal! I'll help you up! Let me help you!"

Michael, still smiling, acquiesces, unfolding his legs so I can pull him to his feet. The minute he's standing, I push him back over the arm of the couch. "There!" I say. "How do you like that? What do you think of that? Ha!"

Mike grabs for my hands. He wants to do it again.

"What's the matter?" I say, full of fake sympathy. "What's wrong, little guy? Want me to help you? Let me help you! I'll help you up! See?"

I help him to his feet and then push him down on the couch again. Mike squeals with joy, grabbing at my hands again.

We repeat this five or six times before I try to change the game.

"You want to go for a walk?" I say.

Mike doesn't say anything. He seems to be considering what it is I might be saying.

"Hike?" I say. "Want to go for a hike?"

Silence.

"Okay, Mike," I say. "I'm going to take that as a yes. We're going for a hike. Okay? We're going for a walk. Put on your shoes please. Can you put your shoes on? They're over there. By the door. Put your shoes on. Okay? Good job, Mike."

"Anyone want to go for a hike?" I shout in the direction of the stairway.

I get no response. "Hey!" I shout, poking my head around the corner into the dining room. Sam is at the table reading a book. "You want to hike?" I say. "In the woods? With the . . . sticks and . . . stuff?"

No response.

I return to Mike and help him with his shoes. Then I track down d'Artagnan's leash, and we're ready to go. Mike is dressed in his stretchy shorts and his T-shirt with a lizard on it. D'Artagnan is leaping and leaping.

"Hey!" I shout again. "Boys! Answer me!"

"What?" says William, slamming open his bedroom door.

"We're going on a hike," I shout up the stairs. "Out on the . . . trail. You know. Like we used to?"

"Yeah?"

"Yeah."

"Have fun!" he says.

"How 'bout you, Sam?"

Sam glances over the edge of his book. "You going to buy me lunch?" he says.

"I just made lunch!" I say.

"That was *salad*," he says.

"Where's Lucy?" I say.

"Over at her friend's."

"Well," I say, "we're going. Tell Lucy. See you guys later."

It's too late. Everything is too late. I've already lost them. They are moving away from me. I wonder where they are going.

I open the passenger's side door for Mike. He climbs in. I walk around to the driver's side. Climb in. Start the truck.

Before the twins were born, when Deb, Sam, William and I were living in University of Iowa family housing, I'd bundle the boys in their snowsuits, load them in the double stroller, and take them on night walks. Up the hill toward West High School. "Maybe you'll go there someday," I'd say to them. William, the younger and louder of the two, would usually fall fast asleep within the first few minutes, the bright stars overhead and the traffic noise from nearby Route 218, but Sam would stay awake, leaning forward as we walked toward Mormon Trek and beyond, sometimes all the way to the Finkbine golf course parking lot, the nylon ropes pinging against the aluminum flag poles, the first and tenth tee boxes and white fairways falling away into the night. He'd point at things and name them. Snow. Flag. Golf. Car. And I'd praise him for being so smart. The next spring, the boys and I explored the dry creek bed between family housing and the cornfield directly adjacent. We found an old mattress down there. And the remains of a campfire. We invented stories about a gang called the Midnight Murderers. The dry creek bed was their clubhouse. I remember telling the boys stories about the Midnight Murderers. We became, in the stories, members of the gang. Sam, by his choice, was called Football Pad. And William, by my choice because he couldn't talk, was called Round Head. My name was Frankie. In the stories, we had all kinds of adventures. One time, we climbed all the way to the top of the radio tower we could see from the cornfield and stole the blinking red light. Everything we did was cool. And the boys wanted to spend time with me. But no more. No more gangs. No more adventures. I guess that's what happens when kids grow up. It would be pretty weird, after all, at their age, me leading them down to a dry creek bed and telling them stories about the Midnight Murderers.

Last year, Deb found three beer cans in Sam's closet. We grounded him. A few months ago, she found a bag of marijuana in the same spot. We grounded him again and took away his Xbox for a month. I told him his phone was next. This is the only way we could think to handle it. Punishment seems to be all we have left. Sam doesn't care about praise anymore. Not, at least, our praise. Maybe we already used up our quota. When he was a baby, we'd praise him for everything. He was hungry, and we'd praise him. "Good job! You're hungry!" He'd eat, and we'd praise him. "Good job! You're eating!" He'd poop in his diaper, and we'd praise him. "Nice work! What a great poop you made!" He'd scribble a little picture with crayon. "What an amazing work of art!" we'd say. Now Sam and I are no longer on the same team. He drinks beer, and I do not praise him. I punish him. He smokes weed, and I punish him. I should be worried about his substance abuse, and I am. But I worry more about his choice of hiding places. Or I should say "hiding place." I wonder if we will ever be on the same team again. I wonder how he will ever make his way in the world if he can't even be bothered to find a decent hiding place for his weed and alcohol.

The leaves are thickening, most of them just now making the turn from light green to a darker, more solid color. It's a warm and sunny day and the forest is just the place to be. The sunlight through the leaves makes the paths at Squire Point glow with a magical light, making it easy to believe in impossible narratives and unearthly superpowers. Mike takes every opportunity to sit down, while the dog, excited, pulls ahead enthusiastically. Mike is feeling the smooth clay on the side of the trail.

He rubs his cheek on the smooth clay. Feels it with his lips. Rubs it with his hands. Presses his entire body against it. Despite the dire warnings on the signs at the entrance to the trail, I let the dog off his leash. He dashes, unbridled, through the magical underbrush, stopping here and there to inspect wonderful things. Mike is feeling the clay. There is no need to feel anything else. Because there is enough in this clay, in this little patch of clay, to hold Mike's interest forever. It's smooth, for one. It's smooth like someone's skin. And it's brownish red in color. And, if you look closely, you can see that there is moss, which is dark green and very soft like someone's hair, and the moss is just starting to grow along the edge. And there are dry, brown leaves. And if you look up, like Mike is doing, you can see that the leaves produce strange shadows when they move. Strange shadows. And here and there, for brief moments, you can see the sky. Which goes on forever.

Every now and then, d'Artagnan comes sprinting back to me to prove what a good dog he is, and then he sprints away again.

"Come on, Mike," I say. "Let's walk."

Mike doesn't want to walk. He's very happy not walking. But I have told him to come on. And I have said it in an authoritative voice. And he wants to make me proud of him, so he walks. The dog, back on the leash, continues to pull ahead. Despite the pinch collar. It's almost like flying a very heavy kite. I pull back hard on the leash. Mike, holding on to my right hand, lags behind just enough so that when we climb the hills I'm forced to pull him forward. Down the hills, he presses on my hand so I'm easing his descent. The dog doesn't understand his new retractable leash. He can run and run, and then, suddenly, he is forced to stop. He doesn't understand this. It makes no sense to him. The dog goes. Mike stays. This is the dynamic of our walk. After about a half an hour, we come to a thirty-foot-high limestone point and the lake opens up. Someone has installed a park bench so we can sit and watch the pleasure boats chew up the surface of the water and the little Jet Skis spit their rooster tails high in the air. The dog pants like a locomotive. He can't stand it that we've stopped. And even sitting on his haunches, he radiates motion. Mike, on the other hand, has found a stick. He is lying back against my lap gently tapping his stick on a nearby tree branch. The branch is covered with bark that has a fine reptilian pattern. It takes very little effort, if the stick is perfectly vertical, to move it first toward the branch and then back away from it again. Mike smiles faintly. It's brighter here on the point. There are fewer shadows flirting with the light. And there it is: the sky that goes on forever.

"You fell in love," said Deb.

"Yeah. I guess I did."

A jogger puffs by on the path behind us. The boats out on the reservoir are noisy. They tear up the water, accelerating first one way and then another. Some of the boats are much too large for such a small reservoir. I imagine they belong to people from Chicago who are used to much larger bodies of water. Bodies of water that are so large you can't see the other side. Where you can accelerate and accelerate all day long without having to worry about the dinky little Jet Skis and little seventy-horsepower outboards. You can't really see the people operating the boats from the point and I wonder if they're having fun. I wonder if this is the moment they dream about all week. The strong wind in their faces. The hull spanking the surface of the water. The boats move back and forth. They never stop. I wonder where the people live. I wonder where the boats are going. I wonder why they never stop.

I have moments of being in love with my wife. Familiar flashes of memory. Like snapshots. Road signs flipping by. Pages. Crooked fence posts. Rows of snuffed-out cigarettes. Deb on the back of the ST1100. Hands around my waist. Chin on my shoulder. Somewhere in the Midwest, an ancient barn is collapsing, its ridge broken. Its support columns destroyed. "Look," she shouts into the wind. "That barn has fallen to its knees!" She's taking a bath in a cheap motel room in Milton, Vermont. She's sleeping. She's sitting in the middle of an abandoned highway again. This is the image that keeps coming back to me. Weeds have worked their way up between the cracks. There's a dilapidated grain elevator somewhere nearby. Deb's arms are propped behind her. She's looking away from me. Toward the sun. I can't remember the long intervals between the flashes. Just the flashes. I guess that's all my life has been. Flashes. That's how I've loved Deb. In flashes. Here and gone. Maybe that's all it's been. Things we have lost. Like our future. The thing that once seemed so full of promise. And then, for the past ten or twelve years, was so solid and nailed down that there seemed no way we could escape it. Just one more thing lost to the flood.

The lawyer, Deb told me, said she should expect about two thousand six hundred a month. Plus half the equity in the house. She said that this was pretty standard. So, Deb figured, if we could get three fifty for the house, that would leave her with about seventy thousand dollars. Enough to put down on a good place. And with the two thousand six hundred a month plus the money she made from her job at St. Luke's, mortgage wouldn't be a problem. Her real estate agent said three fifty was a good place to start.

At night, I lie down with Michael in the dark. We play a game where he places his hand near mine and I grab one of his fingers. And he struggles to pull his finger away, but I increase my grip pressure. Michael laughs and uses all his strength to get free. After a few seconds of this, I let go. Then Michael places his hand near mine again. And I grab one of his fingers.

Not long ago, it was morning. But that's gone now. Morning can't last forever. That would be absurd. The birds would die of fatigue with all the singing. And nothing would grow properly in that uncertain light. Morning passes. And evening passes. If, late at night, when our minds tumble over and over like laundry in the dryer, we consider what we have done on this day to be stupid, or ridiculous, or boring, or maybe even a betrayal of something vital and sacred in us, we might fall on our knees and clasp our hands together just like someone might do if they were praying. "God," we might say. "Help me, God. Help me. God, please help me."

EVERYBODY PLAYS THIS GAME: If you had (you name an amount of time) left on this earth, what would you do?

Have sex with your wife.

Cook a great meal.

Get drunk.

Smoke a cigarette.

Play golf.

Have sex with someone.

It has been two weeks since the rivers crested. I'm standing on the concrete dock behind the maroon Dumpsters at the Iowa River Power Company Restaurant. Keith is upset because Dave told him to throw out a box of double-A batteries that was ruined in the flood. He brings the problem to Danise, who is Dave's wife and also the owner of the business.

"Dave wants me to throw the batteries in the Dumpster!" he says.

Danise, in the middle of a drag on her cigarette, exhales smoke while saying, "So, throw them in the Dumpster. Where else are we going to throw them?"

"You can't throw *batteries* in the *Dumpster!*" says Keith. He's outraged. "Don't you care about nature?"

Danise takes another drag. "Listen," she says, blowing out more smoke, "nature just flooded my fucking restaurant. I'm not a big fan of nature at the moment. And they don't take them at the landfill. So throw them in the fucking Dumpster. Jesus Christ!"

In the kitchen now: "This fucking thing has been running too cold since you replaced the coil," says Jim, indignantly.

"Really?" I say. "I only heard about it this morning."

"We told Keith *three days ago,*" says Jim. He's pissed off.

The digital thermometer reads eighteen degrees. I kneel and slide open one of the stainless steel cooler drawers.

"It's empty," says Jim.

I remove the drawer and shine my little halogen flashlight beam inside. The fans are running but the cooling coil is a block of ice.

"Bad thermostat," I say.

"Well . . . ," says Jim, shrugging with impatience.

"Okay," I say. "I'll get it. I've got the thing we need in my truck."

The under-the-grill, two-drawer cooler is a pain in the ass to work on because, first of all, it's got a grill on top of it. The grill, being a grill, is usually very hot. There's no way I can lean over it in order to unplug the cooler. Also, the gas piping makes it impossible to move without shutting off the gas and disconnecting the union.

Once I have the union disconnected, I wait for the grill to cool so I can move it.

Everything's covered in grease. Tiny droplets cast off from ten thousand kitchen experiments. This grease, on the whole, smells like Chinese food. Chinese food that has been left in the car for a few days. If you dig around inside kitchen equipment, this Chinese food stench will cling to your clothes and actually enter your skin and cannot be removed with soap or Virginia 10 solvent or any other cleaning or degreasing agent. Unless you consider time a cleaning or degreasing agent.

Time is not the quickest cleaning/degreasing agent to use. But it's the most effective.

Line cooks are not polite. They want to cook. They want to cook steaks and hamburgers and pork chops on their grill. If they can't cook, they might as well hang up their aprons and go home. As far as I can tell, line cooks don't think long-term. Even one day ahead to the big brunch. Their minds work at five-minute intervals. Five minutes; flip the steak. Why, they wonder, is this asshole disconnecting one of our two gas grills? Why is he blocking our way? Why doesn't he get the fuck out of our way?

Joe Blair

I don't want to be here, in the way. I would rather be almost anywhere else. But I can't afford to think in five-minute intervals. I need to look ahead. Thirty days at least (billing cycle). Or a year (parts warranty). Or thirty years (mortgage).

After I remove the still-hot gas grill, pull the grease-covered cooler away from the grease-covered wall, and unplug the cord from the wall outlet, I remove the second drawer and lie on my side on the grease-covered floor and have a look inside. It's very dark inside the cooler. I hold my flashlight in my mouth and crane my neck to point in the directions I'd like to illuminate. My head won't fit inside the cooler, and the cooling coil is far enough back that I can touch it with only one hand at a time. This one-handed work arrangement, along with the lying-on-my-side arrangement, and the holding-a-flashlight-in-my-mouth arrangement makes everything suck. I try to remove the panel that protects the coil and fan motors, but there's too much ice built up. Four days' worth of ice, a bulging, white mass of it. The panel won't budge. The ice, of course, needs to be removed. One method of ice removal, my favorite method, is walking away and coming back to the job the next day. Time will melt the ice. Time will do that. But Jim is pissed off. He wants it now. This is important.

I stand up and dodge two line cooks. I walk out to my truck and retrieve my industrial electric heat gun and heavy-duty extension cord.

The trees along First Avenue are full of leaves. Cars signal and turn. A week ago, the entire strip was underwater. All the restaurants were flooded. All the equipment. All the grease. Everything. The Hardees on the corner of

First and Sixth will be demolished. That's what they say. I wonder where they'll have the classic car rallies now. Maybe at the McDonald's. The Le Chateau Apartments, where I rented a room for my office in the winter and spring of '05, will be demolished. It will be as if these places never were. They say the Lone Star won't reopen. Or the Subway. Or the Taco Bell. Forty percent is the statistic. Forty percent of businesses destroyed by natural disaster never reopen. It makes you wonder whether or not the people running these places sort of wanted an excuse to close them down. Any excuse. After flipping burgers every day. Every day. And hiring high school kids. And hiring high school kids. And flipping burgers. And hiring high school kids.

A flood's as good an excuse as any. Who can say, "You should rebuild your burger joint in that flood plain"? Who could defend such an argument?

The Iowa River Power Restaurant, which, fifty years ago, was an operational power plant, was built directly on the Iowa River. That's part of its charm. People like to eat their steaks and look out at the falls and the dead trees across the river and sometimes the bald eagles that nest there. A section of the basement is a few feet below the water table. It's a big sump; continually flooded with water by design. When, during the last flood, the big electric lift pumps failed, everything on the upper level of the basement went under. Three walk-in coolers and two ice machines and two or three condensing units. Dave and Danise took out a quarter-million-dollar loan to replace the equipment and flooring and walls and ductwork and everything else that went under. Apparently, they didn't want an excuse to close down. They passed on taking the obvious excuse. "It won't happen again," said Dave. "Not like that. It won't happen again like that."

Joe Blair

But I wonder. We've had two floods in the past fifteen years.

Back in the kitchen, I plug in my cord and begin the de-icing process. After about thirty seconds of lying on my side and holding the electric heat gun out at arm's length, my deltoids are exhausted. That's how long I can hold up. About thirty seconds. I steal a frying pan from the grill and place it upside down inside the cooler. I balance my industrial electric heat gun on the pan and let it go. It slides partway down the pan and then stops. I wait, ready to snatch it before it falls into the water. It stays on the pan. It seems solid enough.

To help the defrosting process, I grab my coffee cup and fill it with hot water. Lying on my side, I reach my single arm in, flashlight in mouth, and slowly dump the hot water on the surface of the ice. After about twenty minutes of heat gun and water-dumping, although the ice seems almost unaffected, there is about an inch of water that has pooled in the bottom of the cooler. This water, which has the same Chinese food stink as everything else in every commercial kitchen, soaks the sleeve of my work shirt when I reach in with my quarter-inch spin-tight to try to remove the coil panel. Eventually, the water leaks over the lip at the base of the cooler and onto the terracotta floor tiles where I'm lying on my side. I'm soaking wet with the Chinese food water when, with my elbow, I knock the industrial electric heat gun off the frying pan into the pool of water.

Suddenly the darkness is gone. The little brick house is gone. The kitchen is gone.

But these things, I know, are trivialities.

I am no longer standing. Only sitting in a field. Reclining on my arms like I used to do at the beach. How long ago? There is a blindingly bright light in the . . . not sky, exactly. But I'm not blinded. I am alone, save for the light. Deb is not there. Not that I can tell.

Although I'm aware that I'm in a state less than fully conscious, that anything I might know for certain at the moment will seem ridiculous in five minutes when I'm back to normal, reclining in the . . . not field, exactly . . . once again believing in the logic of things, I think we had it wrong. To the question, "If you had (you name an amount of time) left on this earth, what would you do?" I would answer, "It doesn't matter. In the end, it will be too late for this question."

This has been your life.

These are the things you have done ten thousand times.

And then . . . this is what comes next.

What can the difference be between the death of a single man and the death of All Mankind? There is no difference. One tragedy is no larger or smaller than the other. Not, at any rate, if you're the single man.

The circuit that blows is the same circuit that runs whatever computerized system the kitchen uses to process their orders. Directly after the loud pop, brilliant arc, and smell of ozone comes a ringing and loud cursing from the line cooks and kitchen manager followed by sounds of concern when they see the refrigeration guy lying on the floor.

Idiots die this way. Lying in water. Using industrial electric tools. I am an idiot. But somehow I'm not a dead idiot. Yet.

WILCO IS ON WHEN I arrive at Pamela's for dinner. The house has been cleaned. There are even places to sit. "Sit wherever you like," says Pamela. She is dressed in a white blouse and a pair of dark blue, loose-fitting shorts. It's been a few days since Deb and I had our talk. I should feel relieved. I am free now. I can do whatever I want. I pull out a chair from the dining room table. "Not there," she says, motioning toward the living room. "In there."

I walk into the living room and plop myself on the maroon couch. The old dog in the corner lifts his heavy head off his front paws and looks me over. Then he returns his head to its previous position.

"He likes you," Pamela says, having suddenly appeared in the doorway. She hands me a cold glass of something.

"What's this?" I say.

"Lemonade," she says. "Made it myself."

"Really? Wow. That's cool."

Pamela sits on the couch next to me. Now is when I begin to be nervous. I haven't dated in seventeen years, and this seems, if nothing else, like a date.

"So," I say.

Joe Blair

"So," she says.

"Nice day, huh?" I say.

We both look out the window. The weather has turned hot since the rivers peaked and summer seems to be making up for lost time, providing us with our first prolonged dose of sunlight since last fall.

"Yeah," she says. "Beautiful."

"Yeah," I say.

We continue to stare out the window. Neither of us is a kid. We don't need to make small talk. If we have nothing to say, by God, we won't say anything. We can just sit here and look out the window if we want to. It is a beautiful day, after all.

The short silence seems to last forever.

"Well," I say.

She turns and looks at me. She's looking at me in a meaningful way. Like she knows me very well and I know her very well and we share some deep understanding about something or other.

"I have something for you," she says.

"Really?" I say. "What is it?"

She unfolds her legs and sets her lemonade on the arm of the maroon couch before she stands up. "I'll get it."

I'm relieved when she walks away. But that relief doesn't last long, because she soon reappears carrying four boxes, three things that look like books and one small box on top. They are all neatly wrapped in paper that looks like it has been hand-painted.

"What's this?" I say.

"For your birthday," she says. She sets the gifts down on my lap. "Well, *late* birthday, anyway. I know it was last month but . . ."

"Thank you," I say. "Did you do this?" I touch the hand-painted wrapping paper.

"Yes," she says.

"Wow," I say. "It's beautiful. I don't want to open them."

"Oh," she says, reaching over and ripping an edge of one of the larger boxes, "just open them."

"Are you sure?"

She laughs. "I'm sure," she says.

I gently remove the tape from one of the books and slide it out. It's one of the books she wrote. "Oh!" I say. "Great! Thank you very much!" Pamela is seated next to me again, and I lean over to give her a hug and kiss. And, although we've hugged and kissed before, it's not natural this time. It's something I'll need to work on. The second book is another book she wrote. The third book is a book of poetry by Rumi, which I already own. "Wow," I say. "This is so great!"

"That's Rumi," she explains. "He's a thirteenth-century Persian poet. Persia is actually modern-day Afghanistan. He's really wonderful, Rumi. Timeless."

"That's great!" I say. "I can't wait to start reading!"

"Oops!" she says, grabbing the small box that has slipped down into the crease of the maroon couch. "You forgot one. Here."

"Oh," I say. "Thank you." I straighten the wrapping paper I have already removed from the other three gifts and smooth it. "I'm going to save that," I say. She laughs again. I hesitate to open the small gift. I don't want it to be anything too personal. Even though I believe that Pamela Bell is my new love. And that she has freed me from my previous life. Ever since three nights ago, when I told Deb about Pamela and was thereby banished from the pale yellow house to a couch in Matt Strong's living room, my heart has been a queer mixture of heaviness and lightness. Henry Miller describes his erection as "a piece of lead with wings on it." That's how my heart feels. I know the lightness is only temporary, caused by the cessation of duplicity. There are heavy times to come, but for the moment, everything is balancing out pretty well.

Inside the box is a cheap little hand-painted medal. "Wow," I say, pulling the medal and its chain out of the box as if it were the Hope Diamond. "Wow!" I say again. "This is really nice! Thank you so much!"

"It's my track medal," she says. "State champ. Hundred-meter hurdles. See? I told you."

"Oh," I say, handing her the medal. "I can't take this."

She pushes the medal back toward me. "You have to take it. It's a present. On your birthday."

"No," I say emphatically. Maybe rudely. "You know it's not really my birthday. And I'm not going to take this. Here. You can take it back. I can't."

She does not move to take the medal. "Why not?" she says, her eyes narrowing.

"It's yours," I say. "You did it. Not me. I'm not going to keep your championship medal. Thank you, though. It's beautiful."

I place the medal in her lap. She still refuses to pick it up. She is quiet for a moment and I'm quiet too. Something has happened, but I'm not sure I want to think about it. "But these books!" I say. "I've got some great reading to do! I can't wait!"

Pamela blinks and abruptly stands, clutching her state championship track medal in her hand. "I've got to check on the beans," she says, quickly walking away. I flip open the poetry book and notice that someone named Paul Westlake has written his name and address on the inside of the cover.

Pamela returns to the living room. When I look up, she removes her white blouse. Her breasts jounce as she throws her blouse across the room. Before I can react in any way (not that I know how I would have reacted if I had had time), she bends down and removes her dark blue shorts and her panties. Then she walks over to the couch and sits down next to me. "There," she says. "Now that's out of the way. Thought I'd just get it over with." Although I know that Pamela is nature's child, and although I would sort of like to be more of a hippie than I am, I still don't want to take my clothes off at this moment. But, at the same time, I know I have no choice. My clothes must come off. Because I can't very well carry off the job of sitting here fully dressed. Not with Pamela completely nude. As I stand and remove my T-shirt, I notice that the sun is illuminating her body. She looks warm and absolutely relaxed. I try to relax. I remove my shorts and then my underwear. I think I look relatively unruffled as I throw my shorts in the direction of her shorts. I sit on the couch next to her. Now, I realize, we must kiss. And we must mean it. This is a date, after all. And we're naked. I lean toward her and kiss her. I hadn't really noticed before, but she seems to want to kiss me in a way my mouth is unfamiliar with. She wants to keep her lips inside my lips, so my entire mouth is covering her mouth like some sort of breathing apparatus. I begin to worry that I've been kissing too loosely all these years. I try to tighten up my lips, but it still doesn't seem to work. We're embracing and

Joe Blair

I'm touching her body. Her waist and her hips and then her back. It's a nice feeling, here in the sunlight with the good music playing and the old dog in the corner. I suddenly begin to wonder about the beans. Can beans overcook? I wonder if she really has any dinner cooking at all. But she must have. She wouldn't have lied about dinner.

"Are the beans okay?" I say.

Pamela pushes me back and frowns severely, shaking her head. "Are you serious?" she says.

I force a carefree smile. And then a small laugh. "I'm just kidding," I say.

Eventually, we make it upstairs to her bed. I'm not sure exactly how this happens. I suppose we must have walked upstairs, completely naked. I can't remember who was first and who was second. Anyway, we're in her bed. This is where the serious stuff is supposed to happen. We still haven't worked out the kissing thing yet, but we're trying. We lie there for a while, kissing and pressing ourselves against one another, and I know that, even though to this point my penis has been at less than 100 percent, soon it will rise up the way it always does. Or, I should say, always *did*. I begin to worry. Usually, by now, I'd be set to go. But I'm not set to go. Not set to go at all. The more I worry, the worse I get at kissing and pressing myself against Pamela. I begin to concentrate more heavily on the kissing and pressing, which isn't going to fool anyone. It's like trying to bluff in a game of Indian poker. It doesn't matter what kind of a poker face you have; you can't very well sit there with a deuce on your forehead and raise the stakes with any success. Pamela begins working her way down my chest toward the problem area. I grab her gently beneath her arms and try to force her back up, but she won't have it. I do not want her to go where she's going because if I fail, I don't want to fail while she's so close. "Do you have any protection?" I ask in desperation.

"What?" she says, frowning again.

"Protection?" I say. "I didn't know we'd . . ."

She sighs and shakes her head again. I seem to be disappointing her constantly. "I know it's not PC," she says, flipping her hair from her face, "but I'd rather not use it if you don't mind. I know I'm okay."

"I'm okay too," I say. "I mean, I've been married sixteen years."

This causes another problematic pause.

"Right," she says. "So . . ."

"Okay," I say.

It gets worse from here. At some point, I ask if she has a vibrator lying around somewhere. Afterward, I studiously avoid saying anything like "I'm sorry." I know this isn't the right thing to say. Because I know she'll only say something generous like "Sorry for what?" Or "That's okay. I just wanted to be close to you." And if she does tell the truth, if she says something like "Yeah. That was sort of a bummer," it'll hurt my feelings. "I'm sorry" can't end well. I also avoid saying something like "This never happens to me," because I know it's a cliché. This leaves me with very little to say. It's difficult to make the transition to dinner. We need to walk downstairs all naked and pick up our clothing. The same clothing we tossed aside in such a carefree manner. "I'll go check on the . . . beans," says Pamela. "Okay," I say. "Is there anything"—my cell phone rings—"I can do?"

I dig in my pocket and check the call. It's Deb. I know I shouldn't answer it, and I don't know why I do. Maybe because I've done everything else wrong. I figure I might as well do one more thing wrong.

J OE," SAYS DEB.

"Well, hello," I say. My voice comes out sounding very formal.

"Joe," she says, "are we sure we want to do this?"

I don't respond for some time and she doesn't say anything to ease the silence. Finally, "No," I say.

"Are you with someone?" she says.

"No," I say.

"You're not with . . ."

"No," I say. "Not"—I glance toward the kitchen, where Pamela is supposedly checking on the beans—"at the moment."

"Okay," she says. "You don't sound like you want to talk, but I'm going to say this anyway. Can you listen? Okay. There was a guy. We got him in the ER yesterday. He comes in. Poor old guy. He strokes out on the sidewalk. He's just lying there. And the cops come and move him off the sidewalk. They thought he was drunk or something. But, somehow, this guy makes it into the hospital on his own. And he's not good."

"What do you mean, 'He's not good'?"

"He won't leave the hospital."

Joe Blair

"You mean he's going to die?"

"Yes. He'll die. We'll keep him alive for a while. Not long. Anyway, this guy is wearing some dirty coveralls. And underneath the coveralls? He's dressed in this nice, dark suit with a tie and everything. Doesn't that make you want to cry? He dressed up in his best clothes before the flood so he could apply for work."

"He could talk?"

"Yes. He can talk. Sort of. It's just hard to understand what . . . Just a minute."

Pause.

Rustling sounds.

"Okay. That's better. Sorry. It's just so sad. This guy had owned his own house outright. And, he didn't have any insurance. He lived out of the five-hundred-year floodplain, so he couldn't get it even if he had wanted it. He had fixed up the place. Done all the finish work himself. And, you know the thing he was saddest about? He said he had a whole freezer full of meat. That's what bothered him the most. He's just a little old guy. Cute old guy. He did everything right. Had a job working somewhere. I can't remember where. He told me. Had a job. Bought a house. Paid for it. He did everything the way you're supposed to do it. And he's not the only one. All these people playing by the rules. Doing everything right. That's what I've been trying to do. And you know what? I've been wrong. It doesn't matter what neighborhood we live in or what our friends think of us or what work we do for a living. It doesn't matter, Joe. What matters is love." She pauses here. "What I'm trying to say is, Joe, we can live the way we want to live. We need to live the way we want to live. We can sell this stupid house. This stupid house is like a weight around our necks. Let's get out. Let's go. You and me and the kids. I'm ready. I'll go with you. We can love each other. Can't we love each other? I mean, why are we in such a hurry to give up on each other? I mean, we have time, Joe. We don't need to rush this thing. Here's what I think we should do: I think you should go do . . . whatever you need to do. With that woman. Or whoever. It doesn't matter. You go do what you need to do. Go . . . try to find what you need to find. And if you don't find it, or if you feel like you want to try to find it with me, maybe we can do that. What I'm trying to say is, I think you were right about a lot of things. I never saw it before, but I've been wrong. I always thought it was only you. I thought you were wrong, but now I know I'm the one. I've been a punishing woman. Just like you said. No. Don't interrupt me. Okay? I've been thinking about this. I have withheld myself from you. I have. I haven't really opened myself up to you the way I should. I've always kept something back. I think it has to do with me being a Cancer or something. We retreat into ourselves. That's what I do. I try to protect myself. And you wanted to love me. You did. I know that. But you never had a chance. I'm sorry for that. I'm sorry. I was wrong. I haven't done my part."

Pamela has returned to the living room and is now seated on the maroon couch. I make my way toward the foyer.

"No," I say. "You didn't do anything wrong."

Deb laughs.

"What's so funny?" I say.

"It's funny. Don't you think? You've been telling me this stuff all along, and now I agree and you disagree."

I laugh, although my laugh sounds somewhat forced even to my ears.

"Oh," she says.

"What?"

"You're with someone."

"Um," I say, "not really. She was in the—"

"Why didn't you just tell me?"

"She was in the—"

"So you're with her. Why—"

"I thought you—"

"Can I ask you a question?" says Deb, sighing deeply. "And, just so you know, I'm not angry. Not at all. I'm just curious. Can you . . . ever tell the truth? Can you?"

"I don't know, Deb."

"You don't know? When is it you don't lie, Joe? That's just a question. Is there a particular . . . date or something? Phase of the . . . moon or something? Do you ever tell the truth?"

"Deb," I say, "I'm sorry."

Long pause.

"Well," she says. "I just wanted to . . . I'll let you go."

"Deb," I say.

Another long pause.

"I'll let you go," she says again.

"Don't," I say.

"Don't what?" she says.

"Let me go," I say.

THE DAYS OF THE flood were the most beautiful days. I know it's blasphemy to say this. It's all wrong. How can I say a thing like this when one thousand city blocks in Cedar Rapids were underwater? When the Quaker Oats plant was shut down? When retired people who lived a mile from the Cedar River, so far from the river that they never even had a fleeting thought of buying flood insurance, lost the largest investments of their lives and were forced, in some cases, to live on the street? But it's true. At the very moment the river crested, the sun broke through and the winds died down and there was a blindingly bright lake where a city used to be, with incongruous street signs and tree limbs gracefully surfacing like in that photograph of the Loch Ness monster and rooftops reflecting on the surface of the beautiful, beautiful new sea and houses floating along like swans directly into the railroad bridge near Third Avenue, which collapsed like . . . a collapsing railroad bridge.

News reports coupled the word *disaster* with the word *flood*. Reporters interviewed people who had lost everything. They called these people victims. The use of this term suggests that there is a perpetrator, and who else but the river? It was the river who had broken into their houses and stolen everything and the river must be hunted down and brought to justice. No one talks about the beauty of the thing. And no one talks about the people who were saved by the flood. Who were happy to see it come. Maybe it's not right talking about things like this in the wake of a natural disaster. Not when there are so many victims.

Pamela is waiting for me at Starbucks. I remove the photograph of her vagina from my glove compartment and drop it into the trash can on the corner. Starbucks has become our regular meeting place. If we were to remain together, in years to come, we might have referred to it as "our" coffee shop. We've developed a routine. We sit down and open our computers and write for about an hour. Then we read aloud whatever it is that we've written. Today, Pamela writes something about traveling to the Labrador coast. The beach is covered with round stones. There are Celtic singers. And doves fly over the sea. And then, in the end, she is looking out to sea again. Looking out. Looking out at that sea. With all the water and everything. When she's done reading, I say, "Yeah. That was pretty good. I especially like that part where you're looking out at the sea. Again."

"Oh," she says. "Oh. Thank you. So, what do you have for me today?"

"Um," I say. "Before I read, I'd just like to say, um . . . you know . . . I'm going to ask Deb to go away with me for a few days. To New York. Yeah. And I got some people to watch the kids. And I'm hoping I'll be going to New York with Deb. To, um, the city. Yes. And . . . What's the matter?"

"That's quite the . . . grand, romantic gesture," she says.

I shrug.

"Could you leave?" she says, gently closing her computer. "Leave me alone now, please."

"Okay," I say. "I can do that. But . . . I don't know what you—"

"I feel sick," she says. "Please go."

"But you said you wanted me to give my marriage every—"

"Get away from me! Go! Go away!"

I pack up my computer and scuttle away from the coffee shop, the way a cockroach might.

Fifteen minutes later, she calls and informs me that, after I left, she went into the bathroom and puked. "That's how hurt I am," she said. And then she asks me a few questions. Wasn't I leaving my wife? Hadn't I told her I was finished with the relationship? Didn't I say I was done? Didn't I tell her I loved her?

Yes. I did say these things.

Didn't I ask her what she wanted? Whether she wanted to be the most precious person to me? The person I would love above all other people and grow old with?

Yes. I said all of that too.

"How could I have been so wrong?" she says, dazed. "I'm usually good at figuring people out. I can't believe I've been so wrong. How can this be? I thought I could be . . . I wanted to be so bright for you. I wanted to be bright."

"You are," I say. "You are bright. And I'm sorry. I'm sorry. But I think everything has changed. I've changed. And Deb has—"

Pamela snorts.

"Okay," I say. "Okay."

"People don't change like that," she says.

"Like what?" I say.

"Like anything," she says. "People don't change. That's what I believe. You can't go to bed one way and wake up and suddenly be this other person. It doesn't happen. That's just . . . what I believe."

I SNAP OPEN MY PHONE and call Deb. It's not like the old days when I was young and I'd call some girl on my parents' rotary phone. Rotary phones were no good because they gave you way too much time to chicken out. I remember fingering the dial and spinning and waiting and spinning and waiting and spinning and waiting and spinning and waiting and then saying "Oh, fuck it!" and hanging up. With speed dial, there's no time for that. Now it's—

"Oh. Hello. Deb?"

"Yes."

"It's me. Joe. How are you?"

"I'm fine."

"Hi. Anyway, how are you?"

"I'm fine," she says again. "Like I said."

"Good," I say. "That's good. Hey, can you talk for a minute?"

Pause.

"Hello?" I say.

"Hello," she says.

Joe Blair

"Can you talk?"

"Just a minute," she says. I hear shuffling and rustling. "Okay," she says. "Go ahead."

"Okay. Hey, I've been thinking. You know how you said it was okay for me to go and . . . sleep with other people and all that? I was just thinking. I don't think I want to do that. I'm not saying *you* can't do it. I mean, you can go do whatever you want. Who am I to say what you can and can't do? That's not what I'm saying. All I'm saying is, I don't think *I* want to sleep with anyone else."

Long pause.

"Hello?"

"Yes," she says. "Well, that's up to you."

"I know," I say. "I'm not laying the matter at your feet or anything. I know it's up to me. And that's the thing. I'm making my own decisions from now on. I think I've lain too much at your feet as it is. I mean, it can't be all that enjoyable for you."

"You lost me," she says.

"Hello?" I say. "Can you hear me now?"

"No," she says. "I mean yes. I can *hear* you. I just don't *understand* you."

"Like when we bought the house," I say. "I left it up to you. And where the kids should go to school. And what's for dinner and . . . everything. I've left it all up to you. I mean, what kind of husband does that?"

"No," she says. "That's not true. You've been a very good . . . provider."

I snort. "Yeah," I say. "Sure. Anyway. I know I've sucked. I really have. And I'm sorry. But I just wanted to say, I don't want to sleep with anyone else."

"That's . . . up to you," she says.

"I know," I say. "I know. And I'm just telling you. Have you seen Pete around?"

Deb laughs drily. "Yes," she says.

"You have?"

"Yes. I have seen him around."

"Oh," I say. "That's good. So . . ."

"I haven't slept with him," says Deb. "If that's what you're after. I'm not planning on it. It's not in my nature."

"I wasn't asking because I don't . . . think you should . . . do what—"

"Okay," says Deb, with an edge. "You want to come over later?"

"Um, yes," I say. "I would choose to do that. If I had that choice."

Deb laughs again, this time less drily. "Come over at around nine. That's when I try to get Mike down. I've got a bottle of wine. It's that same bottle."

"No way," I say. "*The* bottle?"

"Yeah," she says. "I don't care. I've been wanting to get rid of it anyway. I almost threw it away."

I laugh. "That's . . . ," I say, smiling madly, "that's . . . Okay. But I don't want that. I'll bring some beer or something. You can throw that bottle away. I don't want to drink that crap. Probably tastes like vinegar anyway."

At around eight thirty, Deb brushes Mike's teeth and dresses him in his pajamas with The Thing (Ben Grimm of the Fantastic Four) on them and reads him his favorite Little Golden picture book about Big Joe the Truck Driver and then tucks him in and kisses him good night. At nine, I arrive. I throw a Duraflame log in the fireplace and light it. We have beer. We have three Duraflame logs. And music from Pandora. I choose the Sinatra station. Frank starts in on the old number about having the world on a string. Mike is quiet for a few minutes and then the seizures begin.

Sometimes it's a rogue seizure, rising up out of the water and swamping Mike's brain. Grand mal is the tsunami. Rhythmic motion. Bilateral. We haven't seen too many of them. We usually get the lesser ones. Sometimes in clusters of ten or twenty that are spread out over a few hours. Body twisting like a corkscrew. Eyes rolling up in head. Everything clenched. Bladder losing control. We can hear the seizures coming a few seconds before they arrive. A desperate flutter of sound. It's that note of desperation that tips you off. And if you're fast enough, you can spring up the stairs and reach Mike's room before he falls and hurts himself. You need to distinguish the desperate from the nondesperate squealing and shouting. That's the thing. Imagine a weight lifter trying to bench-press a weight too heavy for him. The bar settles on his chest, and then the noise begins. The grinding of teeth. The desperate gasping and mewling. I try to hold him down, mostly. I take special care with his hands, because he has hit me pretty hard in the past. I try to wrap my arms around his arms and gently lower him down to the floor. I need to lower him because usually, when a seizure is approaching, he either sits up or stands up, so that, when the hard part comes, the twisting and tensing of the muscles, he falls. So, it's important to recognize that first flutter of sound. I hug him. And I say the same thing, over and over. "It's okay, Mike," I say. "It's okay, Mike. It's okay." I say this because the look on his face is a look of absolute horror. Like he's afraid of the demons that grab him the way they do. And twist him. And force these sounds from him.

Of course, they're always with him to some extent. They interrupt him. Amuse him. Annoy him. Force him to repeat words and phrases he doesn't want to repeat. These words and visions that are squeezed out of him like toothpaste from a tube. Out they come. Who knows what they might be. *Ferris wheels. Demolished parking lots. Giant structures with no purpose. Ruined fences. Fantasies puddled with piss and thick with weeds. Staple guns. Trash cans.* His heart beats so hard, you can actually see it wrestle with itself, Mike's entire chest churning with each contraction. Mostly, the seizures come at night, sneaky things that they are. But lately, they've become bolder, coming in the middle of the day. In the supermarket. Mike will clear out the entire fresh vegetable section. At school. We'll get a call. The school nurse will be upset. We'll need to calm her down. These seizures: they're vicious and undeniable things. They can't be ignored or rationalized to seem more civilized than they are. They grind like metal on metal.

After a seizure, Mike collapses. If it's nighttime, he'll go instantly back to sleep. And Deb and I, after applying bath towels to the piss-soaked sheets and throwing the latest soiled blanket down the laundry chute and lifting Mike's legs so that Deb can pull on yet another pair of diapers that he will tear off and discard before the next seizure, will feel our way in the dark back downstairs, hearts pounding, waiting for the next round. It is at this moment, in utter darkness, when Deb and I talk to each other.

"Here's the thing," says Deb. "I feel so guilty. That's a lot of it. I feel so guilty. I feel like I'm supposed to save him. I know you think I shouldn't . . . I know. But I can't help it. I keep feeling like I can save him. And then, when I can't, I feel like a failure. No. Don't say it. I just want to tell you this. Okay? You know all the things we've tried? That diet worked pretty well. For a while. But nothing else seems to . . . and there are so many things out there. Different things. Remember that thing we did last year with the behavior modification? And then he was out of control? And he threw that tray of food at McDonald's? I know. It's sort of funny *now*. But it wasn't then. I was so hopeful then. That's the way I've been. Everything we try. Each thing. I think, This is the thing! You don't know. You're . . . you get to go to work every day. No. I know what you're going to say. But just let me say this. Every time, I think, This is the thing! And then, when it doesn't work, I feel so guilty. I'm just so sad, Joe. I'm so sad. Like, long-term sad. Defeated. Not just now. Not just today. Long-term. I've prayed to God. I've prayed so much. But I don't think it matters. I don't think God cares. I don't. This boy, Joe. This boy is so beautiful. And he's so smart. He is. I know he is. And he's right there. He's so close. But I can't quite touch him. I can't get to him. And I'm afraid . . . I'm afraid he's going to end up somewhere and no one's going to love him. Not like I do. No one else seems to even know he's in there. And you know they'll just drug him up and he'll end up sitting in a chair all day like a . . . like a zombie or something. And he'll be lost in there. Inside himself. But, what do I know? I might be wrong about that. Maybe he'll do even better away from me. You know how he does better at school than he does at home. He's better with Michelle than he is with me. Okay. And you want to hear the worst thing? I can't stand to do therapy with him."

"Therapy?"

"Yeah."

"What do you mean, *therapy?*"

"Therapy. You know. Like what they do in school? We're supposed to present him with those picture cards and he's supposed to make a choice? And then, when he makes a choice, we reward him? That's just one of the exercises. You know. We've done them. But I can't stand it. I can't stand it because I do it and do it and Mike never learns. He just gets worse. It fills me with anxiety. And, if he's supposed to pick a certain color or something, and he picks the right one, like, once out of every ten tries? I make a big deal about it and give him a Starburst or whatever, and tell him how smart he is, and then he never gets it right again. There's no payoff. You know? The whole time, I'm anxious. I feel like I'm failing. No. Don't say it. I am failing. I hate to say this, but with the dog? You know when he was a puppy and we used to tell him to sit and then give him a treat? And I could see him learning, and repeating certain behaviors, it made me so happy. Inordinately happy. Because that's what I don't get with Mike. I used to be so hopeful. But I'm not hopeful anymore. I'm not hopeful. I think maybe I've already given up. And I can't stand it. I can't stand myself for it. And the worst part? It'll never end. Not for him and not for me. It'll never end. Never. Ever."

"Deb, you're just worn out. You can't do it all the time. No one can. These people who help him at school? After they're done, they go home and watch a movie or something. They go on with their lives. They have their own futures to think about. What they'll do on vacation. Whatever. That's why they can be so optimistic. With Mike, I mean. I'm thankful for them. Where would any of us be without them? But . . . you can't beat yourself up like this. You get tired. Who wouldn't be tired? Why don't you go on a trip? Why don't you just go? You need to go away."

"I don't want to go on a trip. I'd miss my children too much."

"Deb . . ."

"What?"

"I'll take care of everything. You need to—"

"It's not about that. I don't *want* to go. I don't *want* to."

Pause.

"I know you mean well," she says. "I know sometimes I'm . . . not much of a wife."

"That's not true," I say. "You're—"

"I'm not," she says. "I know I'm not. And I'm sorry, Joe. I'm sorry. And you get so upset about the way I talk to you or something, and in the past, I'm thinking, Hey, get over it! At least you get to go . . . do stuff! And then you're complaining about our *relationship*? I mean, our *relationship*, for Christ sake? That's like . . . that's a luxury we can't . . . I think I'm getting ready for something. I'm just getting prepared for . . . something."

"What are you getting prepared for?"

"I don't know," she says. "Maybe change. Maybe I'm getting prepared for . . . change."

"Well," I say. "Okay. That's a good . . . thing. Segue. Because . . . I've got tickets to New York."

"What?"

"Tickets," I say. "To New York. And . . . I want to take you to New York."

"Who?" says Deb. "You and me?"

"Right. I worked it out with Michelle and one of the women from the Arc and we're covered for three days. And I called my sister and she said we could stay with her in Brooklyn."

I feel a sudden change in the atmosphere. Like a cold front pushing through.

"If this is too fast," I continue, "I understand. I'm sorry. Maybe you should just go alone, or I'm sure I could get rid of the tickets somehow. They don't even matter. I don't mean to—"

"You got tickets to New York for me? You and me?"

"Yes."

Pause.

"Why don't we go?" I continue, blindly. "It would be . . ."

Deb makes a quiet noise that sounds like "Okay."

"Okay," I say. "Okay. We'll go. I think it will be . . . I think it will . . ."

Deb cuts me off by grabbing me roughly and hugging me. She hugs me hard.

WAITING FOR THE INBOUND TRAIN at the Kings Highway stop, everyone continues to peer in the direction of Coney Island, like kids waiting for a school bus. It's late enough in the day for the tracks to shimmer. The faraway workers wearing orange vests weave in the heat. The approaching headlight blinks. The trees, given the two narrow stretches of land, grow, leaning out over the tracks the way trees do. The gray tiles on the subway platform are cracked and the cracks are filled with black grime. The train squeals to a stop. Most of the doors open. Some do not. Everything is broken here. The woman with the bright pink nail polish covers her face with her hands. She seems to be grieving. The Asian woman does not smile. If you suspect someone of terrorism, reads one of the posters on the subway car, you should call a number just as one thousand nine hundred and some New Yorkers did last year. It makes me nervous when Deb breaks open the map of the subway. She looks like such a tourist. And I, sitting next to her, look like the husband who wants to pretend to be a New Yorker.

"Okay," says Deb after a long while. "Fifteen stops to go."

I nod.

"What's the matter?" she says.

"We know what stop it is," I say. "All we've got to do is wait."

"I like to be sure," says Deb.

I nod. I wish she'd put away the map. I wish she would stop taking pictures of me next to the subway sign. Next to the Times Square billboards. Next to the street vendors.

Earlier in the week, before we left for New York, Deb had been unable to sleep and I told her I knew a surefire way. I rummaged through the junk drawer and produced a few buds of sensimilla wrapped in a tattered sandwich bag.

"Where'd you get that?" said Deb.

"That's the bag we got from Sam," I said.

"Oh no," she said. "You know I don't like that!"

"Deb," I said, "don't worry. All it does is make you sleepy." I carved a pipe out of a small potato with a peeler and we snuck out to the garage to take a few hits. After we got high, we began our evening ablutions only to find that this particular bag of weed was more than we bargained for and instead of becoming sleepy, we threw on some nice clothes, assigned Sam and William to watch Michael and Lucy, and headed out the door for Atlas, a restaurant in Iowa City with an outdoor café where you can watch the drunken college students stumble by.

But on this night, the college students seemed to have some sinister intent and they kept looking at us as if they suspected something and the waitress kept bringing drinks we hadn't ordered and Deb was inexplicably speaking with a southern drawl. "Why are you talking in a southern accent?" I said. Deb covered her mouth with both hands, her eyes bugging out like those of a strangulation victim. "Am I?" she said, horrified, through her hands. "I think so," I said. "Say something."

Deb tried to say something, but now she was laughing too hard. "I don't know what to say!" she said, finally. "You sound like Scarlett O'Hara!" I said. "You do! You sound just like her!"

I don't know how we possibly paid for all of the drinks, but I do remember the alleyway. There were lights that made everything look orange. And when something is already orange, like the façade of a building constructed entirely of orange bricks, and it's nighttime and the orange light is making the orange bricks look like some incredible newfound glowing color, an alley seems like the perfect place to have sex. At least Deb thought so. "Come here," she said. "Come here. Where are you going?" There was a green Dumpster that looked dark orange, and there were rubber bumpers on the loading dock that looked black, and the alleyway was in the shape of an L so we could hide, if not from the security cameras that we gave not one thought to, at least from passersby on the street. I did my best to hold her up, eventually leaning her ass on one of the black-looking bumpers on the loading dock. It was quick and, I think, loud and, within what might have been five minutes, we were walking out of the alley and trying to remember where we had parked the car.

By the time Deb and I were lying in our bed in my sister's apartment in Brooklyn, the first night in the city, we noticed that an objectionable odor seemed to be emanating from . . . somewhere.

"What's that smell?" said Deb.

"What smell?" I said, pretending not to notice.

"That smell!" said Deb. "Is that us?"

"Is it me?" I said.

"I don't know," said Deb.

The source was difficult to determine. The odor was strong and foul, but it didn't stop us from completing our mission. When we were finished, we noticed that we had left a pinkish stain on my sister's sheets. "What's this?" I said.

"I don't know," said Deb.

"It's never been pink before," I said. "I don't think this is good."

"It's like I have an infection or something," she said.

We were silent for a moment. "You didn't bring anything home to me, did you?" said Deb.

"I don't think so," I said.

"You told me you didn't sleep with her," said Deb.

"I thought we—"

"Did you sleep with her or not? Did you bring something home?"

It was a difficult thing to say. Even with all of our newness and generosity, I almost couldn't say it. "Deb," I said, "I did sleep with her . . . sort of. I couldn't . . . really do it. Not really."

"What's that supposed to mean, 'couldn't really do it'?"

"You ever try to put, like, one tube sock inside another tube sock?"

"What's that supposed to mean?"

"I couldn't . . . you know . . . get it up. Not really."

Deb laughed. "I bet she didn't feel too good about that!" she said.

"*She* didn't feel too good?" I said.

"Well," said Deb. "If you didn't *penetrate* her, I think we're fine."

"Well . . . ," I said. "I sort of did. Not really, but sort of."

"I don't think you can get anything unless you . . . ," began Deb.

"I sort of did," I said.

We walked to the subway feeling less than fresh. Despite our showers. The thought of a venereal disease put a major kink in our romantic, postflood love vacation. We wait for the Q train at Kings Highway. Everyone is schoolkids. The tracks shimmer. The workers shimmer. The trees reach out over the tracks. We catch the train and get off at Herald Square. Over our late breakfast, Deb ceases to chew suddenly. "What's wrong?" I say.

"I think I know what it is," she says.

I look at her expectantly.

"You know that night? In the alley?"

I nod.

"Did I ever . . . can you remember me pulling out a"—she leans forward and whispers—"a tampon?"

"No," I say. "I don't remember that."

"I don't think I did," she says.

"And then when we got home . . . ," I say.

"I never did!" she says.

"I thought something was a little strange," I say.

"I can't believe you couldn't *feel* it," she says.

"Well," I say. "It's not exactly like my dick has little hands on it or something!"

"It's still *in there*," she says with awe and horror.

"That's why it was *pink*," I say with awe and horror.

We both breathe.

"That's kind of gross," I say, covering my eyes.

"I know," she says, laughing. "How are we going to get it out?"

"I don't know," I say. "I could try."

"How big is a vagina?" says Deb.

"I don't know," I say. "I don't think it's that big."

"I think I might have to go to a doctor."

"No!" I say. "That's crazy! We can do it!"

"I'm going to call Bess. She'll know." Bess, our neighbor when we lived down on Normandy Drive, happens to be doing her residency at the university hospital. Deb dials her number, but no luck.

We reach Times Square. Deb takes my picture again. There are demonstrations going on. Something about the war. There are people selling things, CDs and tickets. There are street vendors and serious-looking people. Finally, Deb gets in touch with Bess. "It dips down," says Bess, "and then comes back up. It's probably hiding behind the cervix. You should be able to get it out."

Deb and I keep walking. Down the stairs into the subway. Back to Brooklyn. On the street again. Weeds grow between the cracks of the sidewalk. I hold Deb's hand. She stops and kisses me. We embrace. "You were right," she says. "You've loved me so well. You have. You've loved me so well. I want to love you like you've loved me." She embraces me. Her body, in contrast to Pamela's, is small and slender. Her breasts are small. Her waist is slim. She seems tiny. I can feel her heart beat.

"I wanted to be so bright," Pamela had told me. "I wanted to be bright for you."

I hold my wife in my arms. We hold each other on the street corner. We kiss like young people. A group of young people stare.

"They think we're having an affair," I say.

"We are," she says. "Aren't we?"

Deb and I stop for lunch at a place in Flatbush. The big football game between Germany and Spain is on. Everyone is interested. I order two drinks. Deb returns from the bathroom. She is glowing. "Got it!" she says.

"You got it?" I say.

She nods.

After dark, Deb and I meet my sister at Coney Island, the famous wonderland that reminds me of a Bruce Springsteen song. *"Sandy, that waitress I was seeing lost her desire for me."*

My sister points out the old parachute ride. "That hasn't run in years," she says.

"What about this?" I say, pointing to a miniature Space Needle–type ride.

"Oh," she says. "That goes up and turns around and you get a good view of the city. But it's broken now."

Coney Island smells like piss. We walk out past hundreds of trash barrels to the ocean. The water is cold. The waves lap against our feet. My sister points out a deserted section of the amusement park. "That used to be Playland," she says. "But it closed down. You can still see the sign, though." The waves lap against our bare feet the way waves do. The Wonder Wheel turns slowly, stopping and starting. It's the highest Ferris wheel in the world. This according to the hand-painted sign near the entrance to the ride.

"I spoke with her last night, she said she won't set herself on fire for me anymore."

The lights do tricks. The waves come slowly. Everything has been destroyed. Things get destroyed all the time. That's the way things are. The carnival rides are rusting. The steel is growing older. Soon all of the rides will break down.

Part Four

DEB HAS NIPPLE RINGS. Two golden hoops. When I come home from work, I find her (topless) engaged in some sort of sporting activity with two men (fully dressed in business suits). "Damn," says one of the men, standing too close. "She's good. I can't beat her!"

I nod. "I know," I say, jovially. "Neither can I!"

I know it's a dream when I wake up. In the dim light of the morning, while still under the covers, I become aware of another presence. It's Deb. She's preparing for work. She walks, wrapped in a bath towel, to the closet. She drops the towel and then glances in my direction. Seeing I am awake and watching, she turns her back to me. Maybe out of modesty. Or maybe out of a long-held habit of denying me something she doesn't believe I've earned. She lifts her arms over her head and pulls on a clingy chemise. I have never seen a more beautiful tableau. I watch the rest of her routine quietly. Her body has been changing constantly over the past seventeen years. She has given birth to four children. Her breasts have become larger and smaller and now larger again. Her arms and legs have thickened and thinned and thickened. She jokes that I'm lucky because I get to be married to so many different women. All of those different bodies. All of those different breasts and arms and legs.

It's been over six months since the floods. The summer, which turned out to be rather hot and dry, is long gone now. As if it never was. It rained two days last week. The rain froze on the streets and the sidewalks and the lawns and the tree branches and the pine needles and the power lines. And now it has snowed. It's well past Christmas. And New Year's. There's nothing left to look forward to other than the end of winter. Everything is closed down. A thousand power lines were down between Des Moines and Davenport. That's what Joe Winters said on the radio. We lost dozens of large boughs from the century-old pine trees bordering River Street. Our front lawn is covered with pine boughs. The oaks and maples fared better, their leaves not yet out. But the pines, strong in a different way than the oaks, were done in by the ice. I pull aside the window shade and look up into them. They look sad. Bereaved. Having lost parts of themselves.

After Deb leaves for work, I pry myself out of bed, pull on some warm clothes and rubber boots, and step outside to shovel the walk. There is a one-inch layer of ice underneath the snow, which I sprinkle salt on and leave. After I salt the walk, I cut up some of the larger broken pine boughs in the yard with a small crosscut handsaw. I'm stacking them, as best I can, near the street when Lucy comes running out with her coat zipped up over her pink nightshirt and tells me she needs help with the last ingredient in the waffles.

"What's the ingredient?" I say.

"I don't know," she says. "Why do you think I need your help?"

"Okay," I say. "I'll come in after I get this sidewalk done."

"Can I saw?" says Lucy.

"Sure," I say. I hand her the saw.

"What can I cut?" she says.

"Whatever you want," I say. "Just don't cut your*self*."

Lucy crouches down in the slush and takes a few awkward cutting strokes on a skinny little branch. The entire branch sways back and forth with each stroke. I remember trying to saw things like this when I was a kid. The hardest part was holding the branch still. "Here," I say. "I'll stand on it." My weight makes things easier, although her right arm keeps stalling out for lack of horsepower, the sticky pine resisting the little handsaw. Lucy keeps sawing. She tries the two-arm method. She's very determined. She takes her work very seriously. I remain standing on the branch. She finally quits, halfway through, and attempts to break the branch off. But the pine is too pliable. It won't break.

Love can be an extraordinary patience. Love can also be an extraordinary impatience. It can happen in the body and in the mind simultaneously. Like addiction. When people quit smoking, they mourn not only the loss of nicotine but the loss of that moment in the back alley with their Marlboro Light when the wind is blowing. They mourn being in the midst of smoking. And then, the smoking being over, they mourn the waiting for the next smoke. Once you've gotten into the habit of something, you are under the power of that thing. And you want to repeat it. That's what habits are all about. Deb's father, an ex-smoker, says that if he is ever diagnosed with a terminal illness, the first thing he'll do is buy a pack of cigarettes.

The dream comes back to me. The two golden rings. And the men who admired her. And Deb, being so proud that she could not be beaten at whatever game they were playing. My cravings have begun again. It's not the idea of my wife that I miss. It's her. Her body. And the way she talks. The way she laughs. The way her breasts press against me when I embrace her. And something else. Something inside her that goes beyond her. Something that goes beyond everything that anyone could be. Only present when she is present. A thing that, when she is gone, seems to be gone forever.

Deb has been gaining weight lately as all paramedics eventually do. She is becoming more substantial. Yet another woman to love. She thinks I'm being kind when I tell her I don't want her to lose a pound. I tell her she's so beautiful, I can hardly believe it. I'm not being kind. Or political. I'm being grateful. There is no body more beautiful to me than hers. Her body is all womanhood. It is my cure. Not because it's the perfect body. But because it's hers. I want her the way the pine trees in our yard want their limbs back. The way an absent father, twenty years too late, wants a second chance at fatherhood.

The little radio in the kitchen is on the talk station. Some woman is talking about the grieving process. Acceptance, she says, happens almost at once. What also happens immediately is a type of grief that she describes as an acute yearning for the person who has died. Why? Because we miss them.

Lucy kicks off her boots and climbs atop her little wooden platform she uses to cook and wash dishes. "What's 'soft shortening'?" she says.

I grab a stick of butter from the fridge. "Here," I say. "You can use this." She hits herself on the forehead. "Oh!" she says. "I knew it!"

I break the stick in two and place it in a coffee mug. I melt it in the microwave and pour six tablespoons into the bowl. Lucy stirs the waffle batter.

I hear the sound of video games coming from the living room. I hear Mike's vocal gymnastics.

"Hey, boys!" I shout. "I told you to clean up this area last night!"

There is no response.

"Do you boys hear me?" I shout.

The game is silenced and one of the boys shouts that he does hear me.

I step back and take a look through the kitchen door into the living room. Mike is on his hands and knees. The older boys are slouched on the couch. Sam's long hair hanging in his eyes. His complexion bad. William still in his housecoat. They both have that bad-attitude teenage look. Soon, I know, they will be beyond my control. Soon they will be gone from me.

"Clean up now!" I say. "I want everything picked up! I'll do the dishes, but you guys need to straighten everything else up. I want that Risk game put away. And what's up with the toilet paper in front of the fireplace?"

William tells me he was using it to help start the fire last night. I try to hide my amusement. I try to look upset. "You don't use *toilet* paper to light a fire. Okay? You use *news*paper."

I tell them, again, to clean up. "Put everything away. I want this place nice when your mom comes home!" I say. I say it because I want them to learn how to work. I love them. In a patient way. I also say it because I want my wife to be happy when she comes home. I love her. Not in a patient way.

Deb arrives home at midnight. I'm online checking out the results of the Oscars when she walks in. "Guess the best picture," I say.

She is exhausted. She drops her bag in the mudroom and stands in the doorway considering. "I don't know," she says. "What're my choices?"

I tell her.

"There Will Be Blood," she says.

Joe Blair

"No Country for Old Men," I say.

We kiss.

She climbs the stairs and into the hot bath I've run for her. I wait in bed. She brings with her, in the darkness, the scents of Dove soap and baby shampoo. A dark continent. Containing its own secret rivers and inland seas. She slides under the covers. "Good night, Mephistopheles," she says. She leans toward me and we find each other's lips. What I say is "Good night . . . Mesopotamia."

It is possible to grieve for the loss of a thing even as you are in possession of it. To crave the very thing you have been blessed with. Deb rolls over on her side. I remain lying on my back. I don't want to sleep yet. I want to be awake a little while longer.

Sᴀᴍ ᴘʟᴀʏꜱ ᴛʜᴇ ꜱᴀxᴏᴘʜᴏɴᴇ at the high school concert band. There are about seventeen sax players in all. Sam is last chair. He has been last chair ever since he took up the instrument, five years ago. Maybe if he ever practiced, he'd be better. But he doesn't practice. Still, I love attending the concerts. Deb and I sit in the large auditorium and watch it fill up. We see dozens of people we know. There's Jill Ross. (That's Will's mom). And Chuck and Nancy Henderson. (Nancy is a doctor. Thirteen years ago, she was a nurse. I remember her taking care of Sam when he was an infant. She'd come in quietly at night with her flashlight and stethoscope and take his vitals.) And the Novaks (whose boiler I replaced). And the Levys and the Butlers. We know these people. We know their children. The junior high principal is setting up the video camera. A friend of Sam's, a girl named Lorelei, waves to us and then walks up the aisle and sits with us. The band members start to take their places. Deb nudges me and points to a name on the program. Gina somebody. "Who's that?" I say.

"That's the love of Sam's life," Deb whispers in my ear.

"Is that who that is?" I say.

I have heard Sam talk about her. He has loved her since kindergarten. "What does she play?" I say.

"Baritone sax," she says.

Joe Blair

I find her in the back row. She has straight blond hair. She looks small and unremarkable. But then, all the girls look small and unremarkable from where we're seated, far back in the auditorium. Gina: unwitting vessel for so much passion. It makes me smile. So much passion.

The band begins to play. The music is a little clunky. But you can hear the gist of the melody coming through. Outside, the cars in the parking lot tick and cool. Time is passing the way it does. Spring will come soon. The ice will melt. The sky is clear. There are no birds. None coming. None going. The temperature will drop into the teens overnight. A night for music. And applause. In a few weeks the crocuses will come. We'll get a warm day or two. Gina will practice her baritone sax. Sam will not. The geese will pass through. The songbirds will come back. And there will be summer vacation for Sam to look forward to. And golf. And softball. And pizza at Pagliai's. And canoeing on the Iowa River. And camping at Lake Macbride. And other things that people do when they live in one particular place. I can't stop smiling. The music clunks on. Not without its ravishing moments. Its blushing soloists. Its leftover songs from Christmas. Its bows and applause. This is a small town. This is our small town.

A AFTER THE CONCERT, DEB and I grab a booth near the front windows of the newly renovated Wig and Pen. Eight or ten months ago, the water had been about even with the top of the front door. Now everything is new. New tile. New drywall. New kitchen equipment. The table has a new copper surface. We rest our elbows on the copper surface and lean toward one another in order to hear.

"That's what I'm afraid of," Deb is saying. "I don't want to end up like her."

"Jesus!" I say. "This place is loud! Those idiots are shouting at the top of their . . ." I study the shouting people. They're young people. They're not idiots. They seem very happy.

"She's . . . like in her fifties," Deb is saying. "Married twenty years. And now . . ."

I lean forward and watch my wife's mouth.

". . . I don't want to get old and have you fall in love with someone else," she says.

"I won't," I say.

"Will you still love me when my breasts sag "—she pulls down the top of her shirt to reveal the tops of her breasts—"even more?"

"Of course I will," I say.

Joe Blair

"Even when you're a famous writer and these young women want to be with you? For your talent?"

I laugh.

"I'm serious," she says.

Her mouth is full of passion. Her eyes are full of passion. "I'll never want anyone else," I say. "I'll be like that old guy. At that restaurant you used to work at . . . the Bull Run."

"Lee Gercio?"

"That guy," I say. "I'll only kiss my wife. No one else."

"He was devoted to her."

"That's how I'll be," I say.

"You won't leave me?"

"Never," I say.

"We're together now," she says. "Right?"

"Right," I say.

"And you love me, right?"

"Yes," I say. "I do love you, Deb. I'm crazy about you."

"You know," she says, "going through all this stuff? I think it makes us better."

"Me too," I say.

"I mean better than . . . at first, even. Early on."

"Me too."

"It's like we stopped living," she says, "for a while. After Mike was born. We stopped living. And we didn't even know it."

"We were holding back," I say. "For some reason. And now . . ."

"We're new again," she says.

"Yeah," I say.

"And," she says, "if you want to go? I mean, move away—"

"I never even meant that," I say. "I just wanted you to—"

"If you want to move away," Deb continues, "I'll go with you. Wherever you want to go. I'll go with you. I want to go."

"I don't know," I say. "Iowa City's not a bad town."

"I want to go," she says.

She studies me for a few beats. Then she holds up her face in a way I have come to know means that I am supposed to kiss her on the lips. Passionately. If I don't kiss her passionately, she will complain. "That's a kiss?" she'll say. I kiss her passionately.

There is something about the pub. The dim lights. The good jukebox. The color of the beer, the taste of tobacco, the shouting patrons, the alcohol in the blood, that makes everything seem good. Bruce Springsteen sings about girls in their summer clothes. And bicycle spokes. And rubber balls. And the things that make up life. Bruce Springsteen is older than we are, which is a comfort. Bruce Springsteen sings about dust and fire and uncertainty and the edge of town. I pray now, in this bar, that Bruce Springsteen will never give up his dust and fire. That he will never grow old in his soul. Because if he grows old in his soul, I may lose hope.

Joe Blair

Passion is an unstable thing to build a life upon. I know this. The thing we are most sure of, in the darkness and noise of the pub, is the thing that will betray us. Even if we are very careful. Even if we are very stable. The precious thing will bleed out over the cold winters. Or be snatched away in an instant. All we can do when we kiss is to kiss with abandon. Not because it's the smart thing to do. But because it's the thing we're certain of at the moment. And then, when time passes, and we trade in our wings for wheels, it won't be the end of us. It can't be. Not when the girls are combing their hair in the rearview mirror. Not when the screen door is slamming. Our souls, here in this place, are insignificant. And young. Insignificant and indomitable—our young, drunken, idiotic, failing-at-twelve-step souls.

Part Five

"YOU CAN'T THROW THAT AWAY," says William. He is referring to the hand puppet I've just picked up from the garage floor. We call him the naked cop. He once had a uniform, but that was the first thing to disappear. Then the stick broke (the one you use to control his left arm). The naked cop still has his cop hat, though. And the thick, black mustache that, combined with the hat, makes him look like a Village Person.

"I'm not throwing him away," I say, walking along the side of the twenty-six-foot U-Haul truck. William and Lucy tag along to see what I have in mind for the naked cop. When I reach the front of the truck, I shove his naked body (the part where your hand goes), through the grille of the truck. "There," I say. "He'll be our mascot."

William and Lucy laugh. This is why I've done it. I want them to laugh.

"He'll never stay," says Lucy.

"Yes he will," I say, looping the naked cop's body around one plastic section of the grille and wrapping electrical tape around him.

Lucy rides with me in the cab of the U-Haul into Illinois. She thinks she's smarter than Sam and William because, although the Honda Odyssey has a flip-down, flat-screen monitor and a built-in DVD player, it also has Mike. And Mike has the habit, on long trips, after prolonged silences, of screaming suddenly with extreme volume, and every time this happens, even though you're sort of expecting it, your heart stops. Every time. This is a kind of torture and it becomes exhausting.

Lucy and I watch the sun rise over Chicago. The sky looks allergic to the city, its edges dull red and sore-looking. And then the sun pops above the horizon suddenly. And soon after this event, the redness and sore-looking edges are gone, the sky returning to the customary bluish gray and all of the objects on Earth becoming once again solid and recognizable. "When we stop," Lucy says, "I'm going over to the car." I feel a stab of sadness, being abandoned in this way. I had imagined the cab of the enormous U-Haul truck as a cozy place that my daughter might remember someday with fondness. "Okay," I say. "Why?" "Too bumpy," she says. "I can't sleep." "Ah," I say, "but you can sleep! Look at all this room! You can lie down right here and let the road rock you to sleep." Lucy doesn't respond. She has already made her mind up and she doesn't want to hurt my feelings. Neither does she lie down. Neither does she go back on her word. At the rest stop, she jumps ship.

Alone now, I pop in the CD that appeared on the driver's side seat of the U-Haul truck yesterday afternoon. At first, I was sure it was Deb who had bought it for me. She was heading to Best Buy for a GPS and I asked her to pick me up a cheap set of earphones for my old Walkman CD player, having checked out four different audio books for the long drive to Massachusetts. "You get the earphones?" I asked. "Got 'em," she said. "Where'd you put them?" "Front seat of your truck." So, when I found the Bruce Springsteen *Born to Run* CD right next to my new set of Sony earphones on the driver's seat, I was touched. "Thunder Road," I have always thought, is the best song ever recorded. It never fails to light a fire inside me. I immediately popped the CD in the old Walkman and sat in the cab, looking out at the rain dripping from the branches of the crabapple tree on Woolf Avenue and, across Woolf Avenue, to the little rental property with the red Hyundai in the driveway. The opening harmonica riff starts like a slowly turning machine, slightly out of balance, then gains speed and evens out. That little riff somehow gets right to the core of me, the love of life and the freedom of it. "Deb," I said, cornering her in the kitchen, my eyes glowing with tears, "that was so sweet of you! And significant, too! I mean, I was just sitting in there thinking of us— the way we came out here with nothing and we're going now with pretty much the same thing . . ."

"We've got four children," she said, sounding insulted. "I think that's—"

"I know," I interrupted. "I know. I'm just saying. All I'm saying is thank you. That was very thoughtful of you."

She looked at me with snake eyes.

"That was very sweet," I pressed on, trying to soften the expression on her face. "To buy that Springsteen CD."

"I didn't buy you any CD," she said.

"You did too!" I said.

"No," she said, shaking free of me. "I didn't."

"Are you messing with me?" I said.

"No," she said. "It was probably that succubus, Pamela Bell. Have you been in contact with her?"

Thunder Road is Route 80. And all the power I need is beneath this dirty hood, the hood of my rented truck. And it is fuel-injected and stepping out over the line. And we're doing it. One little decision. A few phone calls. And we're gone. It doesn't seem possible. We've changed our lives. For better or worse. We've changed. This is not a vacation. This is not make-believe. This is real life. This is Deb and me: jobless. And our four children: at the mercy of a landlord for the first time in over a decade. This is idiocy. This must be what youth is like.

At a rest stop somewhere in Ohio, I notice a man who seems to be enjoying the act of drying his hands too much. He's looking up and closing his eyes, his large hands thrust beneath the hot air of the dryer, triggering and retriggering the automatic sensor, keeping the fan running. If I didn't have Mike, I'd be frowning at the man. I mean, look at him! Why is he standing there when other people need to dry their hands?

When he is finally done with the hand dryer, he snaps into focus suddenly, withdrawing his hands and turning abruptly toward the tiled hallway that leads to the rotunda and the McDonald's. I watch him. Not because he's a novelty. But because I love the man. His untucked shirt. And the way his baseball cap has been sloppily thrown on his head. And his ungainly, lumbering way of walking. He leans against the tile wall as he walks. The tile wall must feel good. It is smooth and yet there are lines in it. He continues, incrementally, to lean more and more heavily against the wall until finally, as I'm done drying my hands and am walking out toward the rotunda, he stops walking altogether and is again closing his eyes, this time with his head down, facing the floor, lost in some kind of reverie. This man very well may be high. Or mentally retarded. Or addled in some other way. But he does not look afraid. And I hope he is not afraid. I hope he is unaware of how he differs from the other motorists who simply wash their hands, then dry their hands, then walk out to the rotunda, and then walk out to their cars, the way I'm walking out to my car, and drive away.

There was a guy at the bar last night, a lounge located on the bottom floor of the Big Ten Motel right off the exit to Route 80 in Coralville, who sneezed loudly. "Wow," I said. "You okay?"

"Yeah," he said.

"Got that one out of your system," I said.

"I don't think I'll ever get it out," he said.

"Really," I said.

I didn't know what he was talking about and I didn't especially care. But in a few seconds, I could see what he meant. He was winding up for another sneeze but, with what appeared to be a great effort, he fought it off.

"Really," he said.

He explained to me that he had fought in Desert Storm and that he had been wounded. I noticed, then, the way his forehead didn't look quite right. That the lines weren't worry lines, but scars. He sneezed again. He went on to explain that he had been with a certain airborne unit and was now suffering from a certain type of lymphoma that affected his spinal column. He sneezed again and introduced himself. I can't remember what his name was. He went on to tell me that he was originally from Boston. That's why he got the tattoo on his forearm. He showed me the tattoo. It was from the rock group Boston's first album, with the guitar that looked like a spaceship. "I was going to get the whole thing done," he slurred. "There was going to be one guitar back here and one here and they were all taking off, and the earth right there exploding, but . . . it hurt."

"Really," I said. "It's a beauty. How much?"

"A hundred and fifty," he said.

Joe Blair

"Wow," I said. "That's a good deal."

He went on to introduce himself again and tell me again that he had fought in Desert Storm and how he was from Boston. Although I noticed that he had a southern accent. I'd guess Arkansas. I told him that I was from Boston too and in fact, early tomorrow morning, I'd be waking up and driving back there for good. He told me he thought that was cool and then he introduced himself to me once more. I shook his hand for the third time and patted him on the shoulder with an open hand. Like I imagined another soldier might do.

Somewhere in Ohio I sent a text message to Peter Lawler. "Thanks for the CD," I texted. It was a shot in the dark. But a few minutes later, I got a return text: "It's a town full of losers," it read, "I'm pulling out of here to win."

The woman on my GPS tells me to continue 257 miles along Route 90 through New York. This makes me smile. Because I know that once I'm through with New York, the only state I'll need to contend with is Massachusetts. And Massachusetts is just a dinky little state. And it also happens to be our new home.

IT'S WINDY IN THE PARK. William can't get a spiral on the football and he's angry that my throws are perfect. "You want to switch sides?" I say. "It's a lot easier over here. It's like throwing downhill." The wind is directly at my back. With very little effort, I'm throwing bullets. But William won't switch sides. He'd rather teach the wind a lesson. A school of yellow leaves falls from the trees surrounding the swing set and jungle gym, and when I catch the movement from the corner of my eye it's as if the entire earth were moving and a dizziness lurches in my stomach. The yellow leaves are just the beginning of a mass migration from tree to ground. I stop in the middle of a throw so I can admire them: the yellow leaves. The wet streets. The hunched and slouching houses dressed in pistachio, dull pink, and white along Elm Street. Fall time in New England lives up to the hype. If nothing else does, fall time does.

West Newton is a cramped little town like most towns in Massachusetts, roads wandering here and there, never bothering with right angles or straight lines. It's part of what makes it home. It's confused and anachronistic and mean and breathtakingly beautiful when the wind blows in October. William and I, competing with one another for the perfect spiral, aren't paying close enough attention because, when we look around, Mike has walked through the gate and is riding a plastic horse which is mounted on what appears to be a compression spring for a locomotive. Michael and the plastic horse are drooping down like an oversize sunflower on its stalk. The sign on the chain-link fence reads "Playground Equipment Built for Preschool Children," but Mike can't read. Not so anyone would know. "Mike," I say, running after him, "you can't get on there!" I grab him and try to lift him off with a bear hug, but he won't let go. He begins laughing. "Come on, big guy!" I say. "You're too big! Let's go!" But Mike is enjoying the attention too much. He clings to the handgrips and laughs.

"First one to get it through that hole wins," says William, pointing at one of the Habitrail plastic pipes meant for preschoolers to crawl through. From this angle, it's a slim ellipsis.

"Okay," I say.

William throws the football. He misses badly.

I retrieve the ball and try. I also miss badly.

"That's hard," I say.

"Let me see that," says William, grabbing the ball.

Mike has become bored with the spring-loaded horse and has moved to the slide, where he is lying facedown, his feet hanging over the top and his head at the bottom. "Look at him," says William, laughing. "He takes up the whole slide!" Mike is a giant in the land of the little playground equipment. He feels the bark mulch with his lips. He grabs a piece of mulch right next to a support pole and pops it in his mouth.

"Augh!" says William.

"That's awesome," I say. "I'm sure a dog hasn't pissed there."

"Get that out of your mouth!" shouts William.

"Don't yell at him," I say. "It's all right. It's already in there. He's not going to swallow it."

Mike chews the bark, smiles, and prepares to swallow it.

"Spit that out!" I say. "Mike! That's gross!"

We move on when we spot a woman and her toddler approaching. The woman looks put out to see us in the annexed zone. William points at another sign as we leave the gated area. It reads "No Ball Playing."

"Huh," I say. "That's Massachusetts for you."

"It's a beautiful house you got us," I tell Deb when we return from our walk. Deb had flown out a month earlier and rented the place. And it is a beautiful place. A three-story gem with fancy woodwork and bay windows.

"It's the fillet of the neighborhood," says William. This is a joke. It's from a movie we saw together a few years ago.

"You don't like it," says Deb, turning from the potato and leek soup she's making.

"I like it," I say. "It's beautiful."

"You don't love it," she says.

"I do," I say.

"Then why are you acting that way?"

"What way?"

"Flat," she says.

I sigh. "I'm not flat," I say.

"You are," she says. "You're flat."

"I'm not flat. See?" I do a goofy dance around the kitchen. "See how happy I am? I'm happy!"

"Don't be that way," she says.

But William, having caught the spirit, dances with me.

"See how happy we are?" I shout.

"Yeah!" says William.

"It's not a competition," says Deb. She seems angry.

William and I stop dancing. "Okay okay," I say. "You win."

Deb turns back to her soup.

William and I wander out of the kitchen and through the door that's off the hallway which leads to the second-story porch. It's nice to have a second-story porch. It's not like a first-story porch because you're not really a part of the street scene. Instead, you're sort of aloof and observing like a second-story god. Not that there's much to observe. The wind has died down now. A mustard yellow Mustang drives by on Cherry Street. A Chevy Celebrity. A mail truck. Some guy is collecting yard waste in shiny black bags, walking from backyard to front and throwing the bags in the back of a U-Haul moving van. The sound of the rear door rumbling shut. The sound of a leaf blower a block away. A white minivan. A red Volvo. I'm close to the electrical lines. Maybe eight feet away. It's strange to be so close to high voltage. These lines are probably about ten kilovolts. That's ten thousand volts. I might, I'm thinking, be able to jump and grab the two lines. It's sort of interesting to think about because the lines look so benign just hanging there, just two little wires, and I'm frightened that I might involuntarily leap out and try to grab them. The girl next door hums a tuneless tune. The houses look beautiful. Every single thing is beautiful. The bushes untrimmed. People live in this neighborhood. They've lived here for three hundred years or so. The cracks on the road have been tarred this spring or last fall by the looks of them. The telephone poles and lines cast shadows across the cracks. An old guy walks past on Cherry, bald on top, arms swinging, hat in hand, blue coat. He is whistling something softly. Somehow a plastic bag has gotten tangled in the branches of a tree across the way. Children are having their childhoods all around here. They'll have memories of sitting on those benches that have been painted so many times it would be impossible for them to rot. They'll remember walking with their moms to that park, where the chain-link is rusting and the stone wall is falling down. The sound of a motorcycle. Birds call insistently. Almost angrily. The sun is strong. It's the first beautiful day. Fifty degrees. Just a slight breeze now. These days. This is the time we have been given. These days. These moments. This is what constitutes what we might call our lives.

Deb is stirring her potato and leek soup. She has left a loaf of fresh bread on the countertop of our new Massachusetts home. And the coffeepot cooling. William and I are on the porch. And if we have time to watch the ruined spiderweb, how it is affected by the slightest breath of wind, how the spider waits on the periphery, ready to retreat into some convenient crevice between baluster and post, and the sparrow fans his tail before coming to rest on the tree branch, and the tetherball hangs from its cord, unused for months at the space of time between one kid poking it around before realizing that tetherball isn't really all that fun and the next kid repeating the same steps and coming to the same conclusion, then this is how this moment of our lives will be spent. It is ours to accept these things or reject them. We may have spirits. We may not. They may flit, when we die, if flitting is what they will do, to one place or another. They may have some knowledge of what we have done here. Walls we have built with the best of intentions. Death, like the flood, might bring some sudden and great insight. Maybe we didn't listen as closely as we should have when a helpless person had something to say. Maybe we were asleep to the intimacies of life when we should have been awake. But these realizations are the province of regret. And I would hope our spirits would be too wise for that. There is, no doubt, enough regret already within us to fill every minute of eternity, but who wants to fill every minute that way? The flood came and it went. You can bet that each molecule of water feels no regret at all about ganging up on the towns and farm fields of Iowa. When was it? Two years ago now? The flood came and it went. And it will come again. The way all messiahs do.

I find Deb in the bedroom. "What's wrong?" I say.

"I don't know," she says.

We sit on the edge of the bed. There isn't anywhere else to sit. Open boxes. Empty dresser. Out the window, the leaves continue to swirl. It's as if we're at sea.

"This house reminds me of a boat," says Deb.

"Really?" I say. "That's funny. Because you said the same thing about the other house."

"No," she says. "I said that was a submarine. But this is more like an ark or something. Don't you think it's like an ark?"

"No," I say. "But it's nice."

"I love this place," she says. "You see all the light?"

"Uh-huh."

"It makes me want to cook," she says. "All this light. I've been living in that dark house for so long."

I slide next to Deb and kiss her on the cheek. She leans in and we embrace. "Thank you, Joe," she says, in my arms now.

"For what?"

"For moving us here. I'm so happy, Joe. I'm so happy. I just feel like . . . I feel like anything could happen here. You know? It was like, we thought it was impossible, and then we did it. Well, we did it, right? That was possible. And I feel like Mike's going to get better. You know how quiet he was on the car trip? He was so good, Joe! He was so happy. I don't think we should let him wiggle the belt anymore. No more belt. I haven't let him have it since he's been here. We've got to engage him more. Don't you think?"

"Yes," I say. "I think you're right. He was just bored. Like you said."

"He was so bored!" Deb almost shouts. She seems to be on the edge of tears again. "Are you happy, Joe?"

"I am," I say. "I'm sorry if I seem flat. It's just I feel a little dizzy. That's all. It's a little scary. I feel like Aeneas with his father on his back leaving Troy. You know? It's heavy."

"We can do it, Joe."

"I know."

"We can. We did this much. We can do it. Mike is going to get . . . Where's Mike? Have you seen him?"

I spring up from bed. "He was downstairs a minute ago," I say, striding to the door. "Mike!" I shout. I listen. From the street, I hear his high wail. I open the door to the balcony and see Mike, bent ninety degrees at the waist, wiggling a belt in the middle of the street.

After the kids are in bed, I set the alarm clock for six in the morning. "Why so early?" says Deb.

"I don't know," I say. "Don't you want to stop somewhere for breakfast before we hit the ocean?"

"Yeah, but we can eat anytime. We don't have jobs. Besides, it's the weekend."

"Okay," I say. "How about seven? Is seven okay?"

"Don't set the alarm," says Deb. "We'll wake up when we wake up."

"Okay," I say, flipping the switch from "alarm" to "off" and unplugging the lamp. The room falls into darkness. Lying on our backs, we can see sudden green stars. Some small. Some larger. Smudges of luminescence. Two shooting stars. Either that or comets, their tails streaking behind them.

"Wow," says Deb. "Isn't that cool?"

"Yeah," I say. "It looks like they did it themselves. I mean, they must have used glow-in-the-dark paint. Right? Because it looks like they were just dabbed on."

"I think so," says Deb.

The fact of the glow-in-the-dark stars tickles me because the house has recently been renovated. All the floors have been refinished and new countertops were installed and the walls have been painted, but the contractor didn't paint this ceiling. Because he had no way of knowing about the stars. We're in our little bedroom. Inside. Looking at the phosphorescent stars above. Thousands upon thousands of millimeters away.

In the morning, Sam finds an inchworm near the trash barrels out back. "Hey, Dad," he says. "Look at this!"

"What is it?" I say.

"Some sort of caterpillar."

I look at the thing. It inches along the way inchworms do.

"Those are probably the things eating all the leaves," I say.

"Probably," says Sam, flicking the worm off his finger.

Time. That's what the inchworm reminds me of. You think it's one way—all stretched out from beginning to end—and then you realize, when time inches along the way it does, it's not that way at all. The middle part bunches up and excuses itself and, before you know it, the head end is pressed right up against the ass end.

Outside, the temperature is dropping. They say it'll get down to the thirties tonight. The wind has abated and the streets are still wet, tens of thousands of yellow leaves trapped there to be trampled by the tires of speeding cars. Soon the winter will come. People will eat fancy dinners and sing songs of peace. You'll be able to see them through the windows. We're people just like they are. We have a home like they do. Soon, we'll have jobs. We'll have jobs in the place we've chosen to be.

P LUM ISLAND IS A barrier island located between the mouths of two
    rivers: the wide, strong Merrimack and the smaller Ipswich. To the
west of the eleven-mile stretch of beach is salt marsh.

"It looks like Iowa," says Sam as we cross the bridge from Newburyport.

"Looks like a salt marsh to me," I say.

"No," says Deb. "He's talking about the color."

Straw brown. Cornfields in late fall, before harvest.

"Yeah," I say. "It's true."

The temperature onshore is in the mid-forties and the water is dark.
I park the minivan in the parking lot on the corner of Plum Island
Boulevard and the road that runs parallel to the ocean along the foreside
of the island. The wind is insistent, pushing us back, away from the water
as we approach.

"This is tight!" shouts Sam. There's excitement in his voice. He's standing
on the edge of the dunes, near the boarded-up snack bar that, in past
summer months, would sell ice cream and Coke and stuff like that. But
it doesn't look like the place has been open for quite a few years now. The
paint is blistering badly and the name on the sign has been bleached by
the weather.

Joe Blair

The beach is narrow today. Almost nonexistent. The storm that blew in two nights ago has reclaimed the dunes that once were thought to protect the houses along the shore. It is as though the dunes have been shorn by an enormous knife, creating sheer cliffs ten or twenty feet high. Two days ago, there were fences that stretched along the tops of the dunes, abutting porches and sliding glass doors, wooden-slatted snow fences supported by steel posts. They are gone now. Cedar stringers are suspended in space, stairways leading down from rear porches and decks into midair. It's obvious that the row of houses (large windows facing the sea, patios and deck chairs, French doors and dormers and cupolas) will go. It's only a matter of time.

The tide is high. With the sheer cliff on one side and the brutal waves on the other and the wind pushing hard from the sea, it's not the smartest place to take a walk. If the tide came in a few more feet, we'd be in trouble. We step over the plastic warning tape with the words "Do Not Enter/ Crime Scene" printed on it. There are six or eight other beachcombers in the narrow strip of sand. One guy walking his two enormous dogs. One woman sweeping the sand with her metal detector.

"Your father took me here on our first date," Deb told the kids after Sam's comment on the color of the salt marsh. "He brought all his dates here."

The boys in the backseat snickered.

"I'm sure he told them all about the little plumbers," continued Deb. "Just like he told me. It was such a good line."

"Little plumbers?" I say.

"Plumbers," says Deb. "The little birds."

266

I laugh, imagining little plumbers nesting in the dunes. "Plovers," I say.

"Plovers," says Deb, unruffled. "They nest here. And they close the beach. The beach is always closed."

The locals have been saying for the last thirty years that the constant pummeling sustained by this island would one day wash the houses on the eastern edge out to sea. The coastline has been eroded by the waves. Pushed back. Someone has built, I see, small jetties, running out a few hundred feet, in an attempt to curb the erosion. They've stacked up sandbags along the shore, much like the sandbags we piled up along the Iowa River in June of 2008, when the floods came. The bags didn't do any good in Iowa. And they're not doing any good here either. "One day, these houses will all be washed out to sea," said the old guy Deb and I rented a cabin from eighteen years ago. It's different hearing it at age twenty-seven, trying to appear to be self-sufficient, than it is when you're almost fifty, walking with your wife and four children down the same beach and all those years are gone. As if they never were. Except for the children and the erosion. And you can see that time has borne the old man out. What he foretold has come to pass. If the houses aren't moved, they will go. And you have to wonder what will happen to the claims the owners have on the property along the beach. What happens to beachfront property when the beachfront disappears? It seems only fair to me, in one way, that the property is simply lost. It's a barrier island after all. The sand that makes it up was stolen from the original shoreline in the first place. Plum Island may have felt clever for a while, existing at the expense of the mainland. But it can't outsmart the Atlantic Ocean. It's on its own now.

Joe Blair

We all limp along the steep incline of the beach. Mike is crying like a seagull, but his mighty cry is swallowed up by the wind and the vast expanse of black, flashing water. He might not exist at all.

Lately the boys and I have been playing the game of what we call the disintegrating man. We start out big, the same way we might talk to someone at a cocktail party we wanted to impress, and we say something like "Hello there. I'm employed as a vice president at Oracle. Yes. I've been there ten years and . . . okay. That's a lie. I haven't been there ten years. I've only been there a year. But I am a vice president and . . . okay. I want to be straight with you. I don't want to mislead you. Actually, I'm not a vice president. The guy who puts the instruction packets inside the boxes of software? That's what I do. It requires a certain amount of . . . all right. That's a lie. I don't work at Oracle at all. Actually . . ." And it goes on until we're jobless and homeless. Without friend or family. Nothing at all. We have repeated this game five or ten times in the past two days, three or four times last night when the car was towed and we had to walk three miles to pay the fine. We were mole men. We were the devil. We were car salesmen. We were many things. But eventually, we always ended up as nothing.

"Your father and I kissed each other for the first time outside that restaurant," Deb told the kids on the way in. "That restaurant right there." She was pointing to the Grog, a small pub down a twisting brick street. "And when we kissed? The minute we kissed, the church bells rang."

"Is that true?" said Lucy.

"It's true," said Deb. "Isn't it, Joe?"

"It's true," I said.

The seas are three to four feet due to high winds, but it doesn't bother d'Artagnan. He retreats when the time comes to retreat, and advances when the time comes to advance. That's the way you need to negotiate waves when you're a dog, since your nostrils point straight ahead. You don't want to go diving into waves headfirst unless you want a snoot full of salt water. After a brief foray into the water, d'Artagnan runs along the shore, where the sand is hard-packed. He's still very fast, even though he's not what you'd call a puppy anymore. There seems to be no real distinction, for him, between the water and the land. He sprints along the beach and into the water, swimming, splashing, running again along the beach, trying to catch some ghost of his puppyhood. There is no hesitation before he goes from shore to surf. No last-second cringe. He just goes.

Sam and William and Lucy and I are hanging back while Deb and Michael, about fifty yards ahead, set the pace. I've got one arm slung over William's shoulders. Sam is walking close on my other side. Lucy is trying to force her way in between us.

"Get out of here!" says William, shoving her. "We're talking about things that happened before you were around."

"Hey," I say. "Let her in."

"But, Dad," says William. "She—"

"Remember that time we went to that seafood restaurant on the Cape?" I say.

"And William freaked out and we had to get the food to go?" says Sam.

William claims to remember it, although, at the time, he was only a baby. "But why did I freak out?" he says.

Joe Blair

"You were just a baby," I say.

Lucy pushes her head under the crook of William's arm. He puts her in a headlock and wrestles her gently to the ground. At this, Sam and I decide to attack William at once. I'm trying to pry William's arm from Lucy's head when I hear Deb's wild shouting. "Joe!" she shouts. "Joe! Help me!" I can see, from my position atop William, that Mike, fully clothed (fleece coat and hat and boots) is walking directly toward the surf. He looks like Frankenstein's monster when he first discovers light, slightly off balance and leaning forward, drawn by a strong force. "Joe!" shouts Deb again. She's gripping Mike at his belt and is pulling with all her might. Mike is laughing. I can see him. Leaning forward. Nearly soaked by an especially big wave. He's winning the tug-of-war. He will walk into the cold Atlantic. He has an idea it will be a certain way. But it won't be the way he thinks it will be. I break free from the boys. Now I'm running as fast as I can in my work boots and finally reach Mike and Deb. Now Mike has gone spaghetti legs and is lying in the wet sand. The next wave may be big enough to reach him, and if it does, and Mike gets soaked, the whole trip, the packed lunches, the quiche we bought at the bake sale, the hour-long drive up to Newburyport, will end. Because Mike will be too cold to continue on our walk. We'll need to get him back to the car. Deb and I drag Mike away from the water. He is laughing.

I look back at the other kids. They appear to be searching for something in the sand.

A couple dressed in L.L.Bean with backpacks and aluminum walking sticks and everything else they might need walks by.

Another couple dressed in black leather.

"There's the black leather couple," I breathe, winded from my run.

Mike is walking between Deb and me now. We are all holding hands. The dog is bounding far off toward the nature reserve.

"I saw the red coat couple a while ago," says Deb.

"And did you see the L.L.Bean couple?" I say, catching my breath.

"Yes," says Deb. "I saw them."

Sam, William, and Lucy are a hundred yards back now. Sam and Lucy are trying to skip stones; William is searching the sand for flat ones. Deb and Mike and I continue on.

We pass a young couple, underdressed for the weather, holding hands.

"First-date couple," I say.

"What are we?" says Deb.

I think about this for a while. "I don't know," I say.

We stop for a little while and look at ourselves.

"So," I say, "um . . . old waterproof golf pants. Mismatching gloves. Um . . ."

"Old boots," says Deb.

"The douchebag couple?" I say.

"*Eccentric*," says Deb, laughing. "We're the *eccentric* couple."

The sea has spit all sorts of plastic items up on the shore. We are never more than five paces from a plastic tampon applicator or a shotgun shell or the lid from a container of orange juice or milk or Pepsi.

A large, black, cube-shaped plastic flotation device of some kind.

A tangle of nylon ropes and lobster markers.

Dozens of lobster markers.

"Look at that," I say, pointing at the lobster markers. "Think about all those lobster traps down there. The traps, they keep on catching lobsters even when the bait is gone."

"Poor lobsters," says Deb.

"They call them ghost traps," I say. "Lobsters just wander in there. And they can't get out. And they just starve to death."

"Is that true?"

"I don't know," I say.

Another shotgun shell.

A nip bottle.

One of those little saw-toothed plastic things from milk bottles.

"Poor lobsters," says Deb again.

Mike keeps removing his gloves and dropping them on the sand. I keep picking them up and putting them back on his hands. He drops his hat. I pick it up and put it back on his head. The next time he drops a glove, I put it in my pocket. Within five minutes, I have both of his gloves and his hat in my pocket. The wind doesn't seem to bother Mike, although his face is bright red. He's smiling and screaming his dog-whistle-pitched scream. A teapot boiling. The waves are furious. It's amazing that the shore can stop them. The wind is constant. The sky is almost always roiling with clouds. There is no color, only black and white and a mixture between the two. Even the seagulls follow this protocol. Black and white and gray. Wide stance for balance. No theories on social justice. The ocean doesn't have any theories either. It doesn't give a shit about the lobsters dying in their ghost traps. Underwater, as they are. Dark and silent, as they are. Trapped in a thing made of harder stuff than they are. It only makes sense they would die. Some states require things called ghost panels to be used on lobster traps that are located off their shores. The idea is, if the trap is underwater for a specified period of time, the ghost panel is supposed to dissolve so the trapped lobsters can go free. I've read that the ghost panels don't always operate the way they're supposed to. We walk along, regarding a series of ruined and discarded things. Broken fences. Black tires lashed together with bailing wire. Broken stairways. Broken docks. Jetties built with granite boulders pointing out into the surf, designed to slow the erosion of the beach. They look silly pointing that way. We all look silly. Walking. Eyeing one another. The plastic debris looks silly. We are all silly. A boy with bright red cheeks. The lobsters caught in traps. And in this way, we all belong. Every bit as much as we don't belong. What I'm trying to say is—beside the ocean, beside the infinite law that water must obey (to seek the lowest level, to obey the gravity of the moon, to freeze and melt and evaporate, to rise up when pushed by the wind, to rage against the shore, to repeat itself incessantly, the same wave, the same wave, the same wave), our laws are silly. I can't help but imagine Barry Bonds hitting baseballs from the shore out into the sea. It would be most unimpressive. I think of Tiger Woods teeing off, the ball flying out to sea. In this wind, two hundred and fifty yards or so. At most. Kind of silly. Steroids. Length off the tee. Marital infidelities. The ocean doesn't care. I think of hydrogen bombs. The end of mankind. Which would affect the law that water must obey not at all. All across the universe, water would still freeze. Or boil. And exist in the way the ocean exists. We pass one more stairway, the bottom step ending about two feet above the existing sand. Michael breaks away from my grip and takes a seat.

"He's tired," I say.

"Let him sit for a while," says Deb.

"You ready to go?" says William.

"We're going to head back in a minute," says Deb.

Joe Blair

"Can we have the keys?" says Sam.

I dig in my pockets and pull out my set of keys. I throw it to him. "We'll be right there," I say.

Deb and I both stand, backs to the wind, and watch Michael. He's happy to be sitting. Looking out, past his mother and father, to the waves. Or maybe he's not looking at the waves. Maybe he's looking at something else. Maybe the clouds, blooming like cauliflower. Maybe some unwritten law. Some code. Some waft of nothing. Whatever it is Mike is looking at, he belongs here. He belongs exactly the way he should belong. Black and white and gray. No gloves or hat. Smiling his eternally mysterious, holy smile. He is my son in whom I am well pleased. Sitting on the bottom step of a ruined stairway. Among the list of things. Plastic bottles. Furious waves. Curling surf. Ribbons of plastic. A woman wearing old boots. Snags of nylon. A boy without hat or gloves. Shredded seaweed. Plastic cigar tips. A man wearing mismatched gloves. Gray and white seagulls on the beach. Seagulls taking off and flying across the water. Seagulls fighting over a chunk of clam meat. Gathering. Eyeing one another suspiciously. Spreading their wings and flying over the land.

It is as though I have been in and out of sleep for years and years. As though I nodded off as a young man and slept through many thunderstorms where the distant lanes roared and the tenpins cackled and finally I have awoken to a world unrecognizable to me, devoid of everything I thought I knew, now trying to recalibrate the laws of physics that seemed, just moments ago, so malleable.

You were right, Deb. I have been nothing. An unread sentence. A secret poem nobody would ever care to discover. I think of James Joyce's snow falling on the dark central plain, on the treeless hills, falling softly upon the Bog of Allen and the mutinous Shannon waves. And the hill where Michael Furey lay buried. I have been nothing. Between sleep and waking. Long away. Deprived of the solid laws that inform the waking world. An object at rest. An object in motion. I have been too long away. Long deprived of that simple thing. That reason. Sam and William are running away along the beach. Not flying, but running. Smaller and smaller as the light washes away over the land, the colors gray and black. Michael, now with his lips to the sand, that wonderful grainy texture, that warmth of the day radiating upward, that distinct thudding and hissing of the salty water advancing and retreating, the whisper of everything unknowable, those secret depths where secret lives are led. The great ocean. Advancing.

If you want, Deb, I will be your shore. You can wear me away. I will be worn away. Gladly. And everything you take from me will be my blessing. Oh, I have missed you! And now, every mile we walk—out to the jetty and back, out to the point, out to that abandoned bench in Rockport where the slats are falling off, the rusting railing, the crumbling granite seawall (myself), while you wash over me again and again—will be my blessing. My blessing. My blessing. I am awake now. I cannot fly. Not in this world. I cannot fly. But I can endure for a while if you are with me.

Acknowledgments

THANKS TO MY READERS—Ian Coonan, Carl Klaus, Joseph Parsons, Ann Bauer, Jay Donahue, Michael Flaum, Jo Ann Beard, Barbara Schuler, Mark Finch, and Cyndi Coyne. You are very dear to my heart. Thanks to my intrepid agent and friend, Janis Donnaud. And Whitney Frick, my editor. Lauren Reece, my writing partner, I am grateful for your presence in my life. Bill Roberts, Carol de Saint Victor, and Mary Allen, thanks for teaching me. Dan Jones, thanks for the break. Bethel AME, thanks for your continued prayers. Mom, thanks for reading all those books to me when I was a kid. Sam, William, Lucy, and Mike, thanks for letting me read (mostly) all those same books to you. Deb, you are my inspiration and my love. I don't think I could couple one sentence to the next without your belief in me. But then, I wouldn't know.

Permissions

A Scribner Reading Group Guide

By the Iowa Sea

—◆—

Joe Blair

INTRODUCTION

In a candid memoir about his struggle to be a loving husband and father, Joe Blair lays bare his dreams and the stuff they're made of. A member of the plumber and pipe fitter union who also earned a master's in nonfiction writing at the University of Iowa, Joe documents his home struggles—a failing marriage, a special needs child, a natural disaster, and a yearning for something new—in his debut memoir, *By the Iowa Sea*. With a genuine narrative voice and an unflinching honesty, Blair documents his journey toward living an authentic life, and the challenges great and small he faces along the way.

TOPICS AND QUESTIONS FOR DISCUSSION

1. Does a place define a family? Discuss the ways in which Joe and Deb give weight to the notion of "home." Consider their first house in Iowa, their youthful motorcycle trip across the United States, and their ultimate move back to Massachusetts.

2. Why do you think Joe was attracted to Pamela? What about her differs from Deb? Do Joe and Pamela just connect over their shared love of writing, or was there something deeper about her being a change from Deb and life at home with the kids? Also, what do you think motivates Joe giving up his affair and attempting to reconcile with Deb?

3. How does the significance of the flood change Joe's perspective? Do you think he finds some personal catharsis in seeing solid places wash away? Why is he so attracted to the deteriorated houses on the beaches of Plum Island?

4. Joe contemplates the notion that all things will be "washed away by time." Do you agree? Is there permanence to notions of love, family, or home? How has Joe's view on this changed by the memoir's end?

5. How does the backdrop of the flooding Iowa River affect the smaller disasters in Joe's life? Discuss how this force of nature plays into Joe's troubles in Iowa. Does the flood also help him somehow?

6. On page 237, Joe writes: "Love can be an extraordinary patience. Love can also be an extraordinary impatience." What do you think Joe means by this? Do you think love can truly be defined as both?

7. Consider Michael's autism and the way it affects Joe's life and

marriage. Reflect on Joe's descriptions of being both awed and frustrated by his son. How did you react to Joe's struggle with raising Michael? Do you understand his actions and feelings? Why or why not? Do you think Michael's return to playing with the belt in Massachusetts nullifies Deb's assessment that he's done better since the move?

8. In reference to Isaac Newton's supposed celibacy, Joe suggests that "what a man refrains from defines him perhaps more clearly than what he accomplishes." Do you agree? From what has Joe refrained, and what has he accomplished?

9. Discuss the games Joe plays with his children: the blinking game with Michael, the disintegrating man with William and Sam, the imaginary personas he, Deb, and the kids take on in the woods. How do these small moments of play reflect on Joe's role as a father? What do these games mean to him?

10. What do you foresee being Joe's greatest challenges in Massachusetts?

11. Consider the clarity Joe experiences when sandbagging. What is it about a simple, redundant process that leads to such self-understanding? How can this notion be applied to his family life?

12. In the same vein, was all that work for naught? As the river waters spread through town, was the communal process of

sandbagging a failure? Is there a point to such simple actions when disaster strikes regardless? How do you justify catastrophe even when you've done all you can to avoid it?

13. Is it the individual moments or the final outcome that defines a life? Explain.

ENHANCE YOUR BOOK CLUB

1. Make a list of the romantic notions you maintained as a child. How did those ideas change as you grew up? Did your life turn out more or less as you planned? Discuss any disasters that might have forced you to change course or reevaluate everything you'd worked for. What are the key moments of your life and love?

2. Read another memoir, such as Jeannette Walls's *The Glass Castle*, Alex Lemon's *Happy*, Abby Sher's *Amen, Amen, Amen*, or Robin Romm's *The Mercy Papers*. Compare and contrast the voice from one memoir to the next. Do they all contain the same amount of honesty and insight? Does a disaster—natural or otherwise—always inform a life and the reflection thereof?

3. Devise a game similar to the ones Joe plays with his kids to play with your book club members. Is there utility in pretending? Are the silly moments created just as important as the ones with more weight?

4. Visit someplace new, a good distance from your home. Can you see yourself relocating to this locale? List and discuss the ways in which a move might change your life as it stands today. Is your city, your street, your house an integral part of your identity? Discuss with your book club.